"Much needed ... relevant and eye-op

HAIRDRESSER OR FOOTBALLER?

Bridging the gender gap in schools

Hollie Anderton
with Ross Morrison McGill

First Published 2018

by John Catt Educational Ltd,
15 Riduna Park, Station Road
Melton, Woodbridge IP12 1QT

Tel: +44 (0) 1394 389850 Fax: +44 (0) 1394 386893
Email: enquiries@johncatt.com
Website: www.johncatt.com

ISBN: 978 1 911382 96 6

Set and designed by John Catt Educational Limited

Reviews

An important book that looks at how gender inequality in society can affect the classroom – and offers clear thinking on what teachers can do about it.

Darren Chetty
Teacher, writer and researcher

For someone who went to a single-sex all-girls school I had the most fantastic education and probably one of the most valuable lessons I took from it was our head's message. She constantly, and consistently, pushed us to believe in ourselves and that there were no barriers to success. Gender was irrelevant to choice. So it does sadden me now to walk into classrooms 20 years down the line and see such a backward careers advice approach in 95% schools I visit. This book will really open the eyes for many to gender gap issues – where they start, the roles we all play and most importantly how we can fix them.

Claire Young
Founder of School Speakers

As a child, I loved acting, singing and painting; but I was made to feel like the odd one out in my school – a highly competitive all-boys' school. I felt the issue, but the other way around. That is why I think that this book is so important. We must all pay attention and take action so that all of our children achieve their potential and follow their dreams no matter what their gender.

Dr Richard Gerver
Author and speaker, expert in Human Leadership

This is a much needed book and complements the work of #WomenEd. The myth-busting sections are very helpful, as are strategies offered to deal with the myths that lead to fixed attitudes to gender. It's easy to read and the voices of teachers and young people mean it is highly relevant – and quite eye-opening at times!

Vivienne Porritt
National leader of #WomenEd and Leadership Expert

Contents

Introduction

This is an important book for everyone involved in education.

When the time arrives for a teacher to work with their students, from the moment a first meeting takes place with a child in reception, or that first day at secondary school, the gender-stereotype damage will have already started; and for the teacher, it's a matter of how much bias needs to be unpicked.

If we are to educate all children, regardless of gender, a shift must also happen with society as a whole. It's a difficult ask and we must also question the underlying habits we have as teachers – habits that may or may not be supporting a gender divide in our classrooms.

At the moment a child is born, their parents may have already determined what colour of clothes the child will wear and what colour the nursery will be painted. Gender research suggests that stereotyping is highly related to children's – and adults' – perceptions of themselves and of gender-stereotyped subjects at school.

From then on, a child's potential may be limited by our bias and a belief that 'boys' and 'girls' should do this and look like that, what colour of clothes they should wear and what careers they should aim for – and those they should avoid.

In this book, Hollie Anderton tackles the divisions associated with gender – not just in our everyday lives, but particularly in schools – and what teachers and school leaders can do to ensure that no individual is limited by their gender. This may be one of the only books to exclusively talk about gender gaps in children and is written by a classroom teacher who truly cares about equality. I am honoured to be able to share a small part in this book.

Throughout the book, the reader will find strategies that can help teachers and school leaders bridge the gender gap in classrooms, playgrounds and in school assembly halls. As Hollie argues, this book will have you deleting the gender column on your data spreadsheet as soon as you finish reading, and rightly so. Together we discuss the inequality, academic differences, aspirations and external forces that all our children have to face, pointing the reader to further research as we go.

The question is, are you willing to tackle the issue straight on? If you're reading this, then you're one step closer to tackling one of society's biggest challenges: gender stereotypes breeding further in our schools – and how we can change the dialogue at the earliest opportunity.

Ross Morrison McGill

Hollie 'Indiana' Anderton

Before you start reading, I want you to think about a couple of questions.

Have you ever been made to feel that you can't do something because of your gender?

If you're male, have you ever felt guilty about your gender because of something someone said? When was the last time you heard someone make a comment about it being a 'man's world'?

If you're female, have you ever wondered what your life would be like if you were a man?

Would your opportunities be different?

If your answer to any of these questions was 'yes', I'm not surprised. While this book is not going to take back those feelings that you've had, it might stop you letting future generations experience gender discrimination. If you've never had those feelings but you can see people who have, then you're brave. You're brave for picking up this book and wanting to make a difference.

No one should have negative feelings about their gender. It doesn't define you. It doesn't make you into the person you are. Just because you're a woman, it doesn't mean that you have to have compassion. If you're a man, it doesn't mean that you have to have strength. Yet these are presupposed ideas as to what makes a man and what makes a woman. Now here's one more question:

Can you remember a time as a child where you wanted to be **something** more than anything?

I can.

I remember watching Indiana Jones running away from the rolling boulder in *Raiders of the Lost Ark*, and reaching out under the closing door to grab his hat just in the nick of time in *Temple of Doom*. I distinctly remember sitting on my red fabric sofa, surrounded by yellow walls, watching the film when it was broadcast on analogue television. It was at that moment that I decided that I was going to be Indiana. Archaeology was all I talked about from then on. Birthdays and Christmas, I was showered with non-fiction books about Ancient Egypt and Ancient Greece, miniature archaeology kits, and I was even bought a pair of khaki trousers for when I went on my real expeditions! I just loved the idea of being able to wear a white vest and cargo pants – while sporting Indy's hat, of course. I loved thinking about leading a team to the greatest discovery that the modern world had ever seen, while still preserving it in its magnificently ancient form. Aside from the adventurer/archaeologist that is Indy, I also found fascination with other archaeologists. Howard Carter made one of the biggest discoveries in the modern world when he uncovered Tutenkhamun's tomb. I would come in from the garden after hours of 'exploring', my knees covered in mud and my face slick with the heat of the British summer. My mum would laugh, 'What are you like!' I didn't think I was like anything, and quite rightly too. Here I was, slaving away in the scorching heat, ensuring that the secrets of the ancient world weren't lost forever, while my parents ensured that I was fed and watered for the duration.

This went on for a good couple of years, until I went to secondary school. One day, I put all of my archaeology gear into a box up in the attic. Why? Because at 12 years old, I was growing up, had a more mature head. I realised that, actually, it probably would never happen. I conjured up reasons in my own head of why I couldn't be what I wanted.

'Well, it's a lot of travelling.'

'Oh, I don't deal very well with hot weather.'

'It's just a childhood fantasy.'

'I'm a girl anyway.'

A girl. Not as strong as a boy. Not as daring as a boy. Unable to cope as well as a boy.

I didn't give it up entirely, though. I took Classical Civilisation at A level, and I still watch documentaries on Egypt whenever they're on television. Every now and then, I go back to my mum's house and dig out the old box full of magazines and little dust brushes. I like looking back at how enthusiastic I was, how eager to be the person to find a tomb that no one else had found. It didn't matter to me at nine years old that all of the archaeologists I had seen and taken inspiration from were all men. That wasn't even nearly a problem.

I'm not trying to show how other people talked me out of achieving my dream. I'm showing how I did it all by myself. I am disappointed to say that I never did become an archaeologist. But I did become a teacher, and with that I can be anything the children need me to be. Even an archaeologist.

I did a presentation on Ancient Egypt in Year 8 and was one of the first to present. As I sat and watched my peers deliver presentations on football teams and cooking, I realised that I wasn't going down the path that was supposedly laid out for me. So, I steered myself back onto the path that was predestined for me as a woman. After that, I wanted to become an actress. I took drama as an option and I made sure that I was the best that I could be. I played powerful women and I played sensitive women. I became different people on stage while keeping my true self reserved for my friends and the people that I felt that I could trust. Drama was an escape for me, and I was someone who loved school.

When I went to university, I carried on with drama, taking it as a degree. Not the most academic of degrees, but it was something that I was passionate about, that I was good at and where I felt most comfortable. I felt confident dressing up and pretending to be someone else; I didn't see that there was any problem with that. Then I faced my own adversities in university. The people around me weren't the same supportive network that I had back home. The students around me came from money and middle-class backgrounds and had very little time for the girl from North Wales. I changed myself, became reclusive, and subsequently left the university I was at to study somewhere else because I didn't feel like me anymore. My gender meant that I was supposed to behave in a certain way, and while there were people like me in university, I didn't fit in with what they classed as normal either. It makes you begin to think that maybe you're not.

The current climate

Even in 2018, gender stereotypes are all around us – this is a sorry state of affairs.

Imagine that you were brought up being told that 'this is for girls' and that some stuff 'is for boys' – and that we shouldn't really cross those boundaries. Unfortunately, due to this limited way of thinking that all generations – including ours – have been plagued with, we are still instilling our children with these thoughts and ideas, however subconsciously.

Gender is a challenging issue. We find ourselves in a world where adults are segregated on pay, job opportunities, and respect based purely on their gender. People we have grown up respecting – those formerly loved in entertainment or in positions of power – are now being revealed as very different people who abuse their power to the point of horror – people that we perhaps wouldn't have listened to if we had known. Before we know it, we are going to be in a world where men and women don't feel as though they can trust each other because all around us, influential people are standing up and saying that what is happening with people abusing their power is wrong, and yet it doesn't seem that much is being done to stop it. This will have a hugely detrimental effect on the children in our care. Some people are standing up because they can see that things aren't fair, that they haven't been fair for a long time. But still for too many people, it's much easier to stand by and watch the world continue to turn in the same way that it always has done.

If you're asking yourself, 'How will this book actually benefit me?', it depends whether you already agree with my views on equality. I am passionate about equality in all manners, and I don't think that children should be made to feel like they can't do anything they set their mind to. If you have a similar mindset then yes, the book probably will help you. Whatever walk of life you find yourself in, you've picked up this book for a reason. Chances are, you've already recognised that change is needed and the purpose of this book is to cement that belief and help you to make that change. We will look at how gender divisions still play a part in our classrooms and how, albeit inadvertently, we are enforcing the belief in children that their future is predetermined by their gender. If, however, you have more traditional views on gender, or if you're one of those who believes that there doesn't need to be any change, then this book will hopefully open your eyes to other perspectives, some that maybe you hadn't considered yet.

Here's the layout...

In this book, we will explore the history of gender equality and then I will discuss three different areas of gender division that I have seen first-hand in schools.

The first section will look at gender inequality through the ages, because everyone likes a bit of history! The book will highlight where there are differences in views throughout the ages and in different cultures. History is crucial; if you know where you've come from, you have a better idea of where you're going. It's important to have an understanding and a respect for everything that has happened to help this cause in the past. In keeping with my love for archaeology, I will even go as far back as the Ancient Greeks. It's worth remembering that we aren't the only people to have fought for equality, so let's do it right.

The second section will explore the academic differences that we all seemingly recognise in children based on their gender. Belief in 'facts' – such as 'girls are better readers', or 'boys are much stronger with their sciences' – are part of the problem that we are facing in our classroom. A look into some real data, and some good old-fashioned myth-busting will have you deleting the gender column on your data spreadsheet as soon as you finish reading. I believe that this is a crucial part to comprehend in order to make a change. If we harbour predispositions that girls aren't going to do as well as boys in maths, then we're hardly setting high expectations for them, are we? Academic differences are something that we have used as a standard in our schools for years. A child who is good at maths shouldn't be a shock just because she's a girl. The same goes for the imaginative, creative child – we automatically picture a Matilda. We are conjuring and imagining these statistics, and all they are doing is creating a divide for our children.

The third section will focus on aspirational differences in children. Aspiration is a huge deal. Take my archaeology: had I been just a little bit more aspirational then I might have become a respected archaeologist in the field of Ancient Egypt. This is one of the most influential factors in how our children think. I got my dream from a film; others get them from looking at their parents or the adults around them. My parents both have your stereotypical 'gendered jobs'. My mother is a beautician and my father is a car salesman. Couldn't get more 'girl'/'boy' than that! However, I've never thought of them as those stereotypes. My mum owns her own business and has worked her way up. My dad is a sales executive of a luxury car brand. That's it. Jobs are what you make of them; if you love what you do and you're forward thinking then any job can be hugely satisfying, and it wouldn't have made any difference to me if my parents had swapped jobs, because they're still my parents. My parents have been successful in their jobs because they love what they do. Children see the adults around them being successful, or not being so successful, and this may have an effect. What shouldn't have an effect is their parents' genders determining what they do. The same goes with children.

The fourth section will address the outside pressures that our children face. We're not so naïve to think that all of the world's problems can be solved from inside the classroom. We know that this battle is far bigger than any of us, but we can do something about it. We can make sure that our children have the best start to life. If we have mastered this in the classroom then that's a solid foundation for other teachers to build on in the future. Unfortunately, some pressures on gender in children don't occur in school. Hopefully, this section of the book will make you aware of outside issues and how you can make a difference outside of the classroom too.

Each section will be underpinned with examples and conversations with real, current children in the education system. It's much more worthwhile asking them directly what their opinions are rather than imagining what you think is best for them, and their responses have made me feel proud to be an educator.

Why me?

This book comes from a deep-seated need for me to help children to grow up knowing that they can do whatever they want to do, regardless of their gender. It has always bemused me that some toys were for girls and some for boys; that boys couldn't read fairy tales and that girls couldn't climb trees. At age 12, I found it astounding that my own brother was laughed at affectionately for asking for a pink pushchair and a doll (that he named Lucy) when he was three years old. Children are the most impressionable beings that we will ever meet. They look to us as adults to help guide them through life so that they can be the best that they can and I can't help but feel that we are still letting them down.

As a primary teacher, I desperately try to bust all of the myths that my children believe about what women and men are able to do. My classes leave me and go to secondary school with a high opinion of themselves and their abilities – why shouldn't they? They work hard for the whole time they're in primary school; they should move on with a sense of pride. They are quick to correct people saying anything derogatory about any gender because they know that they have a great understanding of the idea that gender doesn't matter. The issue that I have – and one of the reasons that I have written the book – is that I'm doing this every year. With different children. All coming to me from the younger years where gender is reinforced in a classroom. It's not intentional and it's not malicious, but it is unnecessary. This book is a toolkit – for educators, parents, and just about anyone else who believes that change is afoot. It's a toolkit to banish gender stereotypes from our education system so that the next generation of leaders can grow up without the restraints that were forced upon us. I don't want any child leaving me giving up their dream like I did. Yes, it was childish, but I still get frustrated with myself for not believing that I could do it simply because no other girls I knew wanted to be an archaeologist. My misconceptions were just that: misconceptions. I could have been an archaeologist; I could have been a spy, I could have been a hairdresser; I could have been a footballer. And I suppose I still could.

For me, this book serves a big purpose: to push for real equality for our young people. We're not too far away now from achieving real goals such as having genderless classrooms, and there's been a lot of work done by other people that have helped the chasm between men and women to narrow. However, there is still a way to go. Even if this book just makes you think about how you treat the children in your classroom whether you mean to or not, that would show that the book is serving its purpose. Children shouldn't be brought up thinking that they are restricted by the gender that they had no choice over. As teachers, we are some of the most influential people in our children's lives. Some feel they can trust us more than they can trust their parents and we spend an awful lot of time with them every single day. What's to say you aren't going to be the person who makes the child achieve their dreams? Even just by telling them that it's okay to be who they want to be. You shouldn't expect to make massive changes in your school but even that one change in your classroom could make a real difference to them.

This book is going to help you make the change that is needed. My aim is that it will make you aware of gender issues that are at play in our education system and give you ways to make others aware too. It will hopefully bust some misconceptions that we have around gender in children and, most importantly, it will supply you with an arsenal of tools that Indiana Jones would be envious of.

Section 1: A history of gender inequality in education

Having attended school in the '70s and '80s, I remember when my friends and I were separated before we had even entered the school gates. One door was the entrance for the boys and another was the entrance for girls. This segregation continued further: not just with entrances, but with toilets and changing rooms. Divisions also existed in the assembly hall. Segregation was woven into the structure of the school building and day-to-day routines. The segregation filtered into some subject teaching. Sex education lessons; gender-biased subjects such as food technology; and sport: the boys would play rugby and the girls hockey. There was no consideration of whether either wanted to do the other!

According to McNaughton (2000), children spend a substantial amount of time attempting to behave like a 'normal girl' or a 'normal boy' and to conform to their own culture's views of masculinity and femininity – with many studies demonstrating that children see our emotions and copy these to express themselves.

How does this unfold in our classrooms? Comments on presentation, hygiene and subject pathways when talking with both genders. How much of this do we support by the things that we say when providing (verbal) feedback in the classroom?

The Bailey Review (2011), *Letting Children Be Children*, set out a list of 'recommendations in relation to the sexualisation and commercialisation of childhood'. It claimed to represent the views of parents on sexualisation and gendered products, and included suggestions such as magazine covers with sexualised images hidden and not easily seen by children, age rating for music videos, and blocking children's access to the internet.

The research considered the views of over 1000 parents with 70 parents taking part in qualitative research and focus groups. 552 children and young people took part. Recommendations exceeded the boundaries of school and the home, calling for the retail industry 'to be "explicitly and systematically family friendly, from design and buying through to display and marketing"' (Barker and Duschinsky, 2012).

The review concluded that there was 'no strong evidence that gender stereotyping in marketing or products influences children's behaviour' and that 'the marketing of pink products for girls could have a positive impact' (e.g. getting them interested in science if it was marketed in pink packaging and related to beauty/pampering). What hope do we have if these are official government recommendations?

Brief overview: a history of gender

Everyone likes a little dip into the history textbooks! We are going to have a brief journey through time to find out just what education was like in 'the olden days', focusing pretty heavily on how gender was viewed by our oh-so-wise ancestors!

Gender divides have been present in societies since the beginning of time. Men and women have always had roles assigned to them, men typically being given more physical elements of work and women there to look after the house and family. It is therefore no surprise that we are predisposed to act a certain way, because that's what society dictates to us. Since the beginning of time, men were the ones who hunted for food and women took the far less dangerous job of collecting things that couldn't fight back for food and warmth while they looked after the children. In its most basic sense, this doesn't seem horrendous and it's not. Men typically are built larger and can therefore complete heavy-duty tasks more easily than a woman. When this becomes a problem is when it is assumed that women are incapable or even unworthy of doing such jobs.

With gender issues having been at the forefront of the societal stage for many years, it's interesting to look back at gender roles over time to see how they have developed. From Ancient Greece, where men were thinkers and workers, to Shakespearean times, where men dressed as women for entertainment, to the female workers during the World Wars, there have always been divides in how men and women were perceived. In this chapter, we will explore the changing attitudes between men and women and how these have helped to reinforce the stereotypes that we see in our everyday lives.

The World Health Organisation defines it in the following way:

> 'Gender refers to the socially constructed characteristics of women and men – such as norms, roles and relationships of and between groups of women and men' (WHO, 2018)

The poignant section of this quote is where it is stated that gender refers to 'socially constructed characteristics'. This would suggest that the characteristics are not biological; they're not natural. In actual fact, they're more like fashioned ideals of what we are supposed to be and how we are supposed to act. This then raises the question: why are we still finding ourselves in a society where if we are not deemed to be acting appropriately to our gender, we are seen as unnatural?

When did it begin to make sense that people can only learn things according to their gender? Surely with the great minds that we've had in our history, someone will have realised that gender is simply not a cause for exclusion. I'm sure that I'm not alone in thinking that these divides are ludicrous, and that something needs to be explored in order for it to be fixed.

When looking at history, literature contains many clues as to where we come from. The earliest texts on education were written in Greek or Aramaic; from these, we can gather some indications of what education was like in this time through the hard work of translators. As we move forward through time, education becomes more refined, curriculum comes into place, and education becomes something for everyone.

As educators, we love showing the children how much education has moved forward and how much it's changed. Many days are spent in our classrooms dressed as teachers and children from times before our own. Imagine the scene. You're completing a topic on the Second World War and you want to spend the day dressed as pupils and teachers from a classroom at that time. What are the children wearing? What are you wearing? Is there a clear divide between genders? It was automatically assumed that the girls would wear dresses and the boys would wear shorts and a shirt. Now, I'm not saying that there is an issue with this. People in those times had their own views and they had societal norms just as we do now. What still astounds me is the fact that we are still conforming to those norms when re-enacting. I'm guilty of having done this myself – until one child in my class was uncomfortable with the expectations of their own gender.

Picture this: a whole day dedicated to acting, behaving and dressing like people from the Victorian era. I was teaching my Year 5 class and (given my background in drama) I thought that it be a good idea to get the children up and involved to visualise what education would have been like then. The children all loved the idea and I was excited about it too. Given that we had been looking at how Victorian people dressed and how they behaved, the children had preconceived ideas about how they were going to dress on this day. This one child came to me at the end of the day after I told them what we were going to be doing and they were in tears. Through clouded eyes, I was asked, 'Will I have to wear a dress?' At that moment, I realised that I had made a slight error in judgement. I hadn't thought about the fact that I should have considered whether some children would feel uncomfortable. I tried to explain to her that she could wear whatever would make her feel comfortable, despite what the other children chose to wear. I almost felt guilty that I had to give this explanation because a child at the age of nine believed that, in order to keep 'in' with what happened at that time, she would have to dress in a way that was not comfortable for her. This piqued an interest for me in the history of gender, especially in education.

This section of the book will focus on gender and equality in education throughout the ages. Children are educated all over the world and, even today, some children are not able to have an education due to cultural and societal norms. While equality in education has come a long way, it's still not at the level that we would expect given the advancements that we have seen in modern day. We would like to think that the days of women being forced to take sewing classes instead of arithmetic are gone; but in some cultures this is still expected, and considered to be normal.

We will now go through different eras in chronological order to explore how education was undertaken and what expectations were given for different genders.

Ancient Greece

In Ancient Sparta, both boys and girls were educated physically. With the belief that all members of society should be strong, there weren't huge deviations between genders here. The belief was held that strong women made for strong children. Ancient Greece was well ahead of the time with their thoughts on education. So what did the great minds of the Ancient Greek civilisation think about educating their young?

Plato

'If women are expected to do the same work as men, we must teach them the same things.'

Ancient Greek philosopher Plato made this statement in the *Republic*, circa 380 BC. It is a show of understanding, of acceptance and of equality. In a world run by men, Plato emerges with a point of view that was forward thinking for his time. Even by entertaining the idea that women *could* do the same jobs as men, he was displaying some advanced views on equality.

While Plato was relatively progressive with his views on gender, he still held the view that women were inferior to men. As a rule, in Ancient Greek civilisation, women were not allowed to take part in anything considered above them (for example, law or politics) but were more suitably placed in the home to look after the family. It is also worth mentioning that while men were regarded as being above women in societal hierarchy, men were not all classed as equals: class and stature played a large part in how much a person could achieve.

Education in Ancient Greece placed a huge emphasis on play – rather akin to our Foundation Stage now! As early as 2400 years ago, Plato himself theorised that children's play could in fact be educational! He puts great importance on the arts of music and gymnastics, leading early ideas that what is good for the body and soul is good for the mind. Having boys learn this was of the utmost importance, showing a world more forward thinking than the world we live in now, completely opposing what we would class as the male stereotype. Girls in Ancient Greece were not permitted to attend school like their male counterparts, but it was thought beneficial to train girls to fight alongside the boys.

Socrates

As the forefather of philosophical thinking, Socrates was the main influence for Plato as a thinker. Socrates believed in educating through dialogue rather than through writing – the dawning of oracy!

Socrates introduced the world of education to the Socratic Method of teaching: asking a universal question and promoting philosophical debate. 'Why are we here?', when asked in my classroom, comes up with some of the most fantastic ideas that I have ever heard.

The philosopher had a great reverence for women, believing that women were equal to men in terms of virtue and asserting that men could not be happy if women were not. Understandably, Plato took on many of his thoughts and beliefs as his own: he was an incredibly influential figure who sometimes opposed the norm. On his philosophical quest, Socrates was faced with charges from the Athenian government for not believing in the gods and for misleading the young people in his care. It's striking how many comparisons we can draw between then and now with people being persecuted for not believing what they ought to in society's eyes.

With these influential men leading generations of learners, it's interesting to look at how their ideas vary from each other and how some are still paralleled today.

Aristotle

'Those who educate children well are more to be honoured than they who produce them; for these only gave them life, those the art of living well.'

This quote reveals some early thinking about the value of teachers. By stating that those who educate children give them a better chance at doing well in life, Aristotle is placing teachers on a higher pedestal than the parents who give birth to them.

As a student of Plato's Academy, Aristotle was in the presence of some of the most incredible minds of the early civilisations. Despite sharing his platform with others who had very different ideas, he had super-clear ideas as to what he thought education should be, and defined the different areas himself. Aristotle believed that there were four main areas of education: reading and writing, physical training, music and drawing.

He also made it clear that he believed these skills ought to be taught at different stages of a child's development in order to create a person with a good moral, spiritual and mental state. This hugely advanced thinking for his time is amazingly still echoed in our teaching over 2000 years later wherein new activities and subjects are introduced to the children throughout their schooling.

Sharing his ideas as to the order of the skills that he deemed crucial, we see our very first blueprint of a curriculum. Aristotle totally understood the importance of having a solid structure and a legislative body to update it.

In terms of his views on gender, he was not as progressive as Plato. Aristotle had firm beliefs that women were inferior to men in all manners. They were simply passive recipients in procreation and were more at risk of danger because of their willingness to succumb to emotion! Given the enormous reach that Aristotle had in his power, it's no wonder that his views on 'the weaker sex' were shared by many of those who studied under him. Just like teachers now, children will believe whatever you teach them, because, being in a position of trust, you're supposed to tell them the truth – it's not surprising that these views are still held by some people 2000 years later!

Roman Britain

After the Greeks came the Romans. The Roman Empire was exceedingly big and therefore had a massive impact on the way the world works, even today. Romans saw great value in education and it's in part due to the Romans that we have the ability to read and write here in Britain.

The initial education system developed by the Romans was drawn from the Greek system that preceded it. The Romans understood the way that the Greeks had taught their youth and understood that it was a well-established programme, leading to some of the best thinkers of the age – clearly they wanted a bit of the action!

The Romans took education very seriously and even the poor often learned the basic skills of reading and writing. Learning in Ancient Rome was very different from modern-day learning. Children would be severely beaten as punishment for things such as being late. The school day was from sunrise to sunset and the curriculum was pretty limited.

And the gap appears again in Ancient Rome when the boys were sent to school (usually at least until they were 14) but girls stayed at home. Some girls were educated to the age of around 11 or 12, but after this age they were able to go and get married so studies that they undertook were more about being a good wife and a good mother. Women were taught to cook and to take care of the household while the men were trained in fighting and public speaking.

'We should not write so that it is possible for the reader to understand us, but so that it is impossible for him to misunderstand us.'

– **Marcus Fabius Quintilianus**

As they built an empire spanning Europe and the Mediterranean, the Romans conquered Britain too. It was at this point that we saw Britain's first recorded education system. Romans were fierce warriors and understood the way of the world.

In terms of school, children were educated to a certain extent. Schooling in Roman times was more accepting than we might first think. The learning was split into three different parts, and these parts were undertaken by children of different statures and classes. At a younger age, children would learn reading, writing and arithmetic; they would then move onto grammar and then further their studies in rhetoric. It wasn't always the case that it was the rich that went to school. It wasn't exclusively for males. While girls would not reach the higher levels of education in Roman society, more often than not they would be able to engage in the first stage of learning. If all the brothers and the family were studying grammar and rhetoric, it wouldn't be uncommon for the sisters of the family to engage in the same learning at home.

As with most societies, the rich and the aristocratic had more of a chance to receive a better education, a paid education.

Grammar in the Roman sense of the word is not massively close to what we would class as grammar now. Rather than understanding what the different parts of language are, the Roman use of the word 'grammar' referred to a course of literature and language, leading onto more oral-focused work so that the students would be able to express themselves in a more eloquent manner.

The Romans brought reading and writing to Britain in 43 AD; until then, there was no such means to be documenting information. It was a huge jump in the British civilisation to now have the skills. Obviously they wanted to share it – and where better place to start than with the youth!

Given that the skills that had been transferred used Latin as the key language, it created quite a job for the teachers at the time, who had to teach every subject as if it were in a second language – which for many it was. Many of the tutors in Roman times were Greek slaves, whose main job was to create more educated scholars to continue the rise of the Roman Empire.

There is not a huge amount of recorded information about Roman schooling in Britain, which isn't ideal; but what we do know is that, having gone through the Roman education system in Britain, one was much more likely to be of a higher rank as one aged!

Medieval Britain

A year that so many of us remember from our own school years, 1066 marked the Norman conquest of Britain. The ambitions of three possible heirs to the throne culminated in a bloody battle near Hastings, with William the Conqueror taking the throne, rightfully or not.

The number of people educated at the time of the Norman Conquest was limited to the wealthy; and even then, not all wealthy people had a level of education. Leading on from the Roman times 600 years prior, schools had been pushed more towards churches and education was in the hands of religion.

The Normans saw a demand for more people to be educated. With trade between countries booming, people needed to understand how to communicate with others in order to keep trade alive. Trade was mainly done in Latin, meaning that lessons had to be taught in Latin too.

This led us to the emergence of grammar schools in England. No longer was it just the wealthy or aristocratic who wanted education to further themselves up the hierarchical ranks; now traders needed some understanding of Latin to be able to trade between countries using a common tongue. Grammar schools provided a way for wealthier trading towns to ensure that their heirs were able to continue trading after they were gone.

Schools in Norman times were exclusively for males. One teacher would teach boys in a single room, often using the older boys to educate the younger due to the lack of resources. Schools were strict and books were far too expensive, so rote learning was the way to go!

It is commonly thought by many historians that all schools were still headed by the monasteries, which isn't the case. The emergence of overseas trade meant that schools were free-standing and set up by wealthy merchants wanting to further the reach of their business by educating the children that they had raised themselves. Schools were no longer exclusively for the wealthy or those wishing to devote their life to God, but they were still virtually exclusively for males.

Where once only priests held the power to be educated and to educate, after the conquest, the Norman monks saw themselves as a higher breed altogether and this led to the decrease in the power of the British clergy being our key educators.

The grammar schools paved the way for access to newly established universities, a surefire way to remain as one of the country's best. The realms of education at all levels were restricted to the upper echelons of society.

Schools were run from sunrise to sunset with breaks throughout the day for meals. A huge focus was put on the ability to read and write – with teachers putting a lot of emphasis on the work of Aristotle in terms of logic. No surprise that such a male-centred education system should choose to teach one of the most chauvinistic Ancient Greeks!

Girls in Norman times had the rough end of the deal. They invariably had one job: to keep a decent household for the husband. Women were not taught to read and write for the purpose of being educated, but rather to stop their minds from wandering and thinking about anything that might be seen as 'unwifely'.

If a wealthy woman's family were to start a school, it wasn't uncommon in Medieval times for a girl to attend this; but outside of these circumstances, it was unheard of. There were massive gender gaps in Medieval Britain, to the extent that women were openly viewed as inferior to men and were there only to serve their husbands and procreate. This is a long jump away from what was once (at least in some part) the somewhat accepting nature of the Ancient Greeks, who first introduced formal education into the world.

An issue that women faced in Medieval Britain was the lack of empathy held by those in charge of the schools. Scholars tended to come from religious orders, all with some damning views about women, typically originating in the Bible. Priests believed that women were below men in all manners. The weakness of their sex dictated that they would not be strong enough to cope with the same level of understanding as their male counterparts. This was not a particularly opposed view and so it stuck around for a long time! While some argued, most didn't. Movement has to be the catalyst for change, and if there is no movement then there's not going to be any change. At this time, there really wasn't much moving. People were settling into their new way of thinking and there just wasn't much thought put into equality.

Tudor Britain

Tudor Britain brought with it a wealth of education growth not seen before in England. With fast-growing grammar schools and the universities having been established for many years, more and more people were gaining access to something originally only meant for the higher classes. Schools in Tudor times reached a new level in terms of more and more people being able to access reading Latin and Greek which meant that it was only really the poor who were left out in the unenlightened cold.

Adults in Tudor Britain saw young people as the next generation. They didn't think of them as children but more like the people who were going to be leading their country in a few short years. It's because of this that they wanted the children to have a decent education to be able to make a decent change to society.

While there was a rise in the number of people being educated, literacy was still the main focal point of education. Rather than giving a full education including advanced maths and science, there was the worry – by many men high up in the education system – that if people knew how to keep their own records or analyse scientific problems, then the limited number of people who could do that was no longer limited. This was an issue because it meant that no longer would people be highly revered for being one of the few trained to be scientists or great thinkers. The children did learn geography and mathematics to a certain extent as they may have been needed in the child's adult life.

Similar to the Medieval British schools, the days were long and the punishments harsh. Boys were expected to attend school from sunrise to sunset and would be beaten with a cane for any discrepancies. With Henry VIII's divorce and subsequent dissolution of many monasteries, the remaining monastery schools had to be covered with money from Henry's own pocket. With the higher-class children being educated privately, the grammar schools owned by the middle classes were growing fast.

Boys went to school at age 4 and then at age 7 moved up to grammar school, where they were taught to read and write Latin – leading on from Roman practice. At 15, when they were deemed to be adult, the boys would leave either to start their professional life or go on to one of the two universities in the country. Both boys and girls were educated until the age of 4, learning the alphabet and listening to the Bible. Brothers and sisters also did not receive the same level of education: a younger sibling wouldn't need to be educated to the same level because the elder sibling already had been. Education was viewed as a way to better yourself, and not everyone needed to reach the same level of education.

Girls in Tudor times were not educated to any great extent. Like their predecessors, girls were educated to a standard that would allow them to support their husband in his endeavours. Some wealthier girls were taught to read at home but it was very rare to see a girl in a school. All girls were taught religion at home, but aside from that, their learning was very limited. Girls were also taught the arts of embroidery, sewing, reading and music to name just a few. These were the skills that were deemed necessary for women to learn in order to keep their household running well and their hard-working husband happy. Echoing the ideas of Medieval times, women were not educated at any higher level due to the fact it might have encouraged them to think outside of their station and get ideas that were classed as above them.

It was also suggested that young boys who were taking part in studies should be taught from an early age by a woman, but that this woman should be matronly and ancient so as not to distract from the learning that needed to take place!

As the Tudor times progressed, girls were more exposed to learning than ever before, being allowed to read and sometimes write in Latin. This gave a welcome break from the monotonous lull of everyday life. It was thanks to Humanists of the time that women were deemed less threatening when educated than first thought. There were some schools that allowed girls in their ranks but many families still did not see the worth in educating their daughter who would marry someone who had enough education for the both of them!

It is interesting to think about the possible views that the children of the era would have had. Did the boys believe that they were superior to girls? Did the girls think it was fair? The answers to these questions would probably never have left the household, for going against what was then deemed as a societal norm would have been hugely taboo. It is only now, in our freer environment that we understand that children have a right to receive answers to such questions.

Georgian Britain

The Georgian period in Britain established a high fashion, high public image, highbrow society. Education in Georgian times led on from Tudor times. There continued to be more and more schools built that allowed for more men to be educated. At this time, literacy rates went up a fair amount.

National education was not yet something at the forefront of government. The church still had control of many schools, with merchants supporting the others. A new ideal of how the public should behave came about in Georgian times. It was no longer seen as acceptable for men to be in any way dependent. It was seen to be super manly if the males were able to refuse help from anyone. This extended to the boys as well: boys were removed from their mother's care and sent to boarding school so that they didn't become too dependent on women. It was the fathers of the families that pushed for the separation to be made, anxious at the possibility that their son might not be viewed as having manliness as a virtue. Women were viewed as eternally childlike. This even extended to the things that they wore. Petticoats stayed with them until old-age and this furthered the general theory that women were inferior to men, just as children were.

This was also a time when there were two distinct spheres separating men and women. Georgian influential figures made it clear that men were to take care of things outside of the house. They were to be the breadwinners and the people who supported their families. The women had to strictly adhere to the rules within the house, similarly to times before them. Cooking, cleaning, sewing and playing the piano made up what I'm sure were pretty monotonous days. This segregation meant that a decent education for a woman was frankly unheard of.

Aside from the social changes that took place in the Georgian period, ideas also changed towards education over time and there was less of a need for girls or lower-status boys to be educated. With wealthier boys, home tuition was a much easier way of learning while the child was still young. As soon as they reached an appropriate age, they were sent to school to live.

There were some shouts for women to be educated, namely to increase their usefulness to society. In some people's opinion, having an educated and devoted wife made one very lucky man.

Given that girls could not attend school, they were sent to something called a 'Dame school'. Dame schools were not true schools but rather places to learn the art of being a good wife. Many women rejected the idea of having to go to Dame school; instead, they took their own education themselves. Learning from siblings or willing parents, women would teach themselves to read and to write in order to feel some sense of being equal to their male counterparts. In Georgian times more than others, women were starting to see that it wasn't fair that only boys were able to better themselves through education. Some of the most influential and powerful writers at the time were women. Jane Austen's heroines were powerful, they could think for themselves and marry who they wanted to marry. They rode horses and rejected suitors. The sad truth of the matter is that Jane Austen herself knew that this couldn't have happened in her reality. Austen taught herself to read and write because her family couldn't afford her schooling. She understood that this placed her outside society's expectations of her gender – and this quite possibly meant that she was seen as an unsuitable wife. A woman who could think and speak for herself would surely end up a spinster in her later life. Women who were educated had to keep their education under their bonnets for fear of being outcast. No self-respecting man would have chosen a woman with an education that could have come even close to his, for fear of seeming inferior (contrary to the beliefs of those campaigning for women's education as stated above).

For the poor, education was a far lesser concern and not seen as very important. The boys would be educated in small schools and not to a particularly high level. The girls would have no education, instead helping their mothers prepare and keep the home for the men. With merchant daughters, it was not considered as important to educate them as it had been in Tudor times, for they could instead learn to help in the business.

Boarding school would consist of lessons in Latin, geography, history, dancing and the classics. The education was not particularly well rounded and meant that people were being left in the dark when it came to scientific advances.

While the social beliefs of Georgian times were developing at an exponential rate, education for women took a real beating and we almost seem to have taken several steps backwards.

Victorian Britain

When Queen Victoria came to the throne in 1837, times were certainly changing in Great Britain. It was the time of the Industrial Revolution, the expansion of the British Empire and a time of clear divide between rich and poor. The education system was no exception to this. The people of the time felt proud to be British, and this was reflected in the ever-growing education system.

Early Victorians felt strongly that education must be a matter for the church, and parents of the children. It was absolutely not a concern for the state, who had far more important things to deal with than something that, in their eyes, was already being taken care of.

But just a few short years after Queen Victoria came to power, the country saw the introduction of the Committee of the Privy Council on Education, a body that would eventually oversee all of the schools in Great Britain. The council offered money to start up schools in impoverished areas, making education more accessible for all. It was seen that education of the masses should be a state concern due to people seeing the benefits of having more highly educated people holding important jobs and so it was established that schools would be erected all over the country to take even the most deprived children.

Here we saw the introduction of ragged schools. Schools that were not merely open to the upper echelons of society, but to everyone who wanted them. They were originally created so that the poor could learn to read the Bible, a small token to ensure that even they would have a chance to enter heaven after death. These schools expanded, supported by the Committee of the Privy Council on Education, so that there were state-run schools all around.

In the 1870s, the country saw the introduction of local school boards. The boards ensured that education was compulsory – and, most importantly, free – for everyone. Whether children wanted an education or not, it was taken out of their hands and the class system became a little more levelled.

Schooling in Victorian times was separated by gender. For boys, the curriculum consisted of the three Rs (Reading, Writing and Arithmetic), history, geography and grammar. Being a strong male was emphasised in these times, with lessons being taught about the 'great men' of the time – something for the boys to aspire to be as they grew up and took their place in society. However, there were separations made from home life. With the strict discipline in school from beatings by the teacher, children began to see their parents as people who deserved the utmost respect as adults. I'd imagine that this created a real conflicting ideology of how children wanted to behave with their parents, and how they were taught they had to. It was thought (and still is to some extent) that strong discipline taught at an early age would make for a more disciplined and aware adult. Boys were subjected to both mental and physical abuse during their time in school – it was not a place people particularly wanted to attend. Education had changed from being in the comfort of our own house with a private tutor or sibling to learn from, to being a military-strict day school where children were punished for not achieving.

Aside from the academic curriculum that echoed that of the Greeks, boys were also taught to converse and dance with girls, in order to equip them for finding a wife as they grew up. Boys were generally taught to treat a woman as if she were a small child, to ensure that nothing too complicated was discussed – for the women couldn't possibly understand. The main difference between boys and girls in Victorian times was that boys had the ability to make decisions, which automatically put them ahead of the girls in their company who were completely incapable of doing such a thing.

Girls were something of a different matter. While day schools were available for girls – a huge step forward – they were taught a very different education, similar to the generations of women that came before them. Cooking, sewing and music were taught alongside the three Rs (same as the boys). The main purpose of a girl's education was to become a good wife, something that I seem to be repeating as I move through this section! Unlike boys, girls were not physically punished; they were far too delicate for this! Women's colleges were opened to allow women to receive formal qualifications to become governesses, in turn pushing forward the idea of women's suffrage – something that was vehemently denied by Queen Victoria. With the advancements that came with this era, women were now allowed to attend university.

The Victorians were certainly responsible for some of the biggest advancements in British society. With the emergence of new free schools, and boards to watch over these schools, education became a staple for all in Great Britain.

Britain at war

The first half of the 20th century wasn't the best of times for Britain. Two world wars within the space of 50 years would inevitably have a huge effect on how the country functioned. World War I – the Great War, the War to End All Wars – was closely followed by an even bigger war, both of which meant a huge loss of British lives. Education was not forgotten about at this time – in fact, it was developed a lot further.

At the beginning of the war, the age for compulsory education stood at 12 years old. After this point, children would leave education for good and choose a trade if they wished to do so. Some would go on to further study but these numbers were not proportionately high. During World War I, schools were visited by government bodies and the findings suggested that schools were hugely underfunded. The end of the Great War came – and so did the Education Act of 1918. H A L Fisher, historian and educator, pushed the idea that putting money into education would ensure the betterment of society, something that a lot of people wanted after the war. The act raised the age for compulsory education to 14 and if students wanted to take studies further, part-time, the age was raised to 18.

Even though the act came in, due to a huge lack of resources after both wars, nothing really changed until after the end of the Second World War. Issues arose with overcrowded classrooms now that state education was available for all. There were not enough trained teachers to cater for all of the new students, many of whom wouldn't have had education in such a formal sense before.

There was talk of introducing a secondary level of education; it was clear that it was desperately wanted by the majority but there was a lot of disagreement on what form it should take. Should it be conducted in the same way as the primary form? Or should the older children be taught differently? This further delayed the progress of developing a secondary system of education.

As with now, schools needed to be at the forefront of decision-making – the driving force behind it, not just the problem.

With state education, all children were entitled to a free education. However, well-educated teachers were more likely to teach in fee-paying schools because the salary was a damn sight better. This unfortunately meant that many brilliant, promising students missed out on what could have been the starting spark of their intellectual journey because they didn't have the same teaching as someone with money.

As far as gender goes, Britain at war brought new ideas to the antique table. While girls were admitted to schools, there weren't as many spaces given to girls than to boys. This was still due to the belief that boys had more important things to learn, and ergo more important things to offer in the long run. The curriculum was split by gender, similar to eras before, where girls learned how to become domestic goddesses, and the boys were taught how to be a man and deal with important 'man-stuff'. One of the most entertaining judgements of the curriculum at the time was that girls were not to be taught maths because it would have no bearing or usefulness in their working life. Given that women were taught to cook, surely measurements should have been pretty high on that list! Which raises the question, did boys learn measures as part of their maths curriculum?

As time progressed, schools branched off into infants, juniors and senior schools. These were open to all students, which was a great jump forward in terms of equality. These secondary schools did widen the gender gap somewhat. Where primary schools were teaching certain subjects to both boys and girls, senior schools taught completely different subjects to boys and girls. This reinforced the beliefs that the woman was to stay at home and that the man was to go out and earn the money for the family. Given what a great effort women put in during both wars, taking control of the munitions factories and joining existing companies to take over the roles of the men, it's bemusing that women were still not seen as equal to men. Many women fought as hard as the men, just perhaps not at the front line.

Women were allowed to attend lectures at university from 1884, but it wasn't until 1920 that one of the most elite universities (Oxford) allowed women to graduate, not just take classes.

Women's rights were a huge topic in between the wars, with suffragettes bringing about ideas that women were worth more. They were faced with some real opposition, and had questionable methods. But with determination and grit, they ensured that women were treated, at least to some extent, equally by means of achieving political enfranchisement. Women finally having a voice in deciding how they wanted their country to be run was a real positive for the fight against gender inequality.

Life for women in Britain was looking more and more fair. Women could vote, become lawyers and vets, and work in government. Education was free for all and a modern curriculum was starting to emerge from the ashes of the broken cities.

Post-war Britain

After the Second World War, times were hard for people in Britain. Suffering massive economic losses meant that we were playing the catch-up game for a really long time. People were eager to get the country back on track by any means necessary, and many looked to education as the catalyst to do this. There were some monumental changes to education from the 1940s to 1988 and these helped to shape the education system that we know and love (most of the time).

There was a big spike in population two years after the end of the war. 1947 saw loads of babies being born and a lot more pressure being piled onto schools in the subsequent years. State-run schools now had to occupy even more students, meaning larger classes and often a less valuable education.

People saw education as a way to boost the morale of the country and stop anything like the world wars from happening in the future. Governments turned their attention to the education system and this meant that the country was braced for much-needed change. These changing attitudes towards education could be attributed to the evacuation process. While it was an awful time for the world, many evacuated children were returning to their urban homes from their time away in rural areas. They came back with a new plethora of knowledge, stemming from the smaller and more intimate teaching found in more rural areas.

In 1944, after much deliberation, the Education Act was launched. The Act introduced the role of Minister for Education – an authoritative figure for schools, ensuring consistency and progress. It established a formal tri-level system where we would find primary, secondary and further levels of education for children.

After some observations on the effects of the Act, it was highlighted that there were huge divides between the social classes and the education that they were receiving. It was suggested that poorer children should be given maintenance grants to ensure that they were being suitably sustained – a far cry from the treatment of the poor in generations past!

Despite the huge leaps made, there were still divides also with grammar schools performing better than secondary schools. It seemed to be that with money comes power, and with power, you could get a better education for your child.

In terms of curriculum, primary education was still massively focused on literacy and numeracy – something that had been the case since the Victorian period. Boys and girls were taught the same curriculum in the same room up until the age of 11. It wasn't thought to bring in any other curriculum subjects due to the fact that they weren't needed until secondary age.

In secondary schools, General Certificates of Education (GCEs) were established in 1951 but there were some teething problems. The papers were marked as either pass or fail, and that was seen as unfair to students who weren't far off the mark. The papers were seen as much more difficult than the ones they had replaced. It was noted that the tests were not catering for the masses like the government had hoped and so the more vocational Certificate of Secondary Education (CSE) was introduced to cater for those pupils who were not, let's say, as academically inclined.

Another teething issue arose with the transition from primary school to secondary school where the jump was proving too much. The idea came about to encourage the building of middle schools. While initially unpopular, these became more and more common throughout the latter part of the 20th century.

In the 1970s recession, people started to look once again at education, noting that it had not, in their eyes, had the desired effect of fixing the country. Accountability for the failings of the education system fell on teachers. This was something that should have been stopped by the people who had taken over the education system – the government. Grammar schools could select their pupils based on sitting an entrance exam, but during the 1970s, the Government suggested that schools should stop accepting pupils based on their academic prowess, but rather more freely. This meant that not all comprehensives performed the worst in terms of national academics. Pupils of all ability levels were able to have access to the same level of education as their peers – something that we still ensure today in most state schools.

The national curriculum was launched in 1987 and detailed everything that schools should be covering to ensure that the country had a solid, consistent approach to skills teaching. The curriculum had a monumental effect on education in Britain – so much so that nearly 30 years later, while the topics have changed with the times, the general gist is very much the same.

A year after the national curriculum hit schoolteachers' desks came the Education Reform Act 1988. The Act took away significant powers from schools but enforced the rigidity of the curriculum and the equality of education for different classes.

Education was almost equal for the sexes. While girls were taught domestic sciences and home economics until 1988, girls did have the same primary education as their male counterparts and the same, to an extent, in secondary school. In secondary school, girls were required to learn home economics and were not allowed to partake in subjects such as woodwork. Boys and girls were taught different sports for physical education. Outside of education, in 1975 it become illegal to preferentially hire candidates for jobs based on gender. The world was moving forward – fast.

Modern Britain

The education world as we see it now is a far cry from the deeply imbalanced gender-biased, classist system that dominated the country throughout history. Today's education system is not as unfair as it was, but it's important to note that full gender equality has still not been reached. As women's rights became more pronounced, more and more women were given the same (or similar) opportunities as men. Lower classes were given equal opportunities in teaching and the poor were educated to the highest levels and still are today. Prejudices in our country lessened and there was a clear understanding for most that education was for the many, not the few.

At the turn of the 21st century, education was equal for all. I started my own education in the mid 1990s, and never had any idea that girls and boys had had a separate and very gender-biased education less than 100 years prior. Never was I made to feel like I wasn't as good as my male peers, or that I couldn't do anything that they could.

Education moved forward very quickly after the Reform. Teachers were and are well-trained by authorised bodies, and stringent checks are made on both teachers and pupils to ensure that consistency is kept. Teachers were moving past Skinner's behaviourism and rote learning into more constructivist ideas based around the work of Jean Piaget. No longer were the ideas of Aristotle, Plato and Socrates taught, but their influence is still around us even now. Educators began to understand the importance of building relationships with the children rather than running their classrooms on fear.

Where once teachers were almost exclusively spinster women, men and women alike are moving into teaching at various stages of their lives. As a young teacher myself, I know that I will get looks from parents who come to collect their child on the first day of school – and the concerned, 'That's your teacher?' in a not-so-subtle whisper because I look young. I also know teachers who entered the profession after doing other jobs for most of their working life. It doesn't matter anymore. Children and teachers alike come from different backgrounds, different places and different times. It all makes for more inclusive and less formal teaching.

Ofsted took its first breaths in 1992 – and weren't all teachers pleased! While Ofsted visits aren't the most happily anticipated dates in the academic diary, they do serve a purpose. Regulations set out by the government need to be administered so that there are no lapses in judgement or attainment in the coming generations. If we take our foot off the gas for even a second then a whole generation could fall down. We, as educators, hold the key to the success of our students and ergo our own future.

Subjects in schools went from being based almost entirely on literacy and mathematics to featuring a wide array of subjects, – vocational included – that mean that our children have the best fighting start in life. Students have a choice over what they learn; it's not all dictated by religion or gender. We plan exciting and engaging lessons where the children can be instrumental in their own learning. We assess; we let them assess; they assess each other. We've learnt that giving responsibility makes for a more engaged classroom; we've learnt that punishment isn't how to get the right answer or right behaviour.

Where the poor would be victimised in terms of gaining a valuable and equal education, we now have schemes that ensure that every family get what they need. Free school meals, CAHMS, and TAC are but a few of the organisations that weren't around when they should have been. We place such an emphasis on the wellbeing of our students, it raises the question of why it took so long for us to realise that they were needed.

After our students leave us, we like to think that they hold a vast knowledge of the world and ambitious, realistic ideas as to what they can be. Girls leave school hopefully knowing that they won't have to spend the rest of their life cooking and cleaning, making sure that they have a well-kept house for their families. Boys will leave school comfortable in the knowledge that they don't have to go into government or find a trade. We live in an accepting society, for the most part, that means that no one but them can dictate what they can do or how far they can go. We hold the power, after so long, to make a real difference to educating the children with this fact. We can be the people that they turn to for advice, not for dictation. Teachers should never take their jobs for granted. While things could still be more equal, we at least have some control over the places that we take our classrooms. One day we can be explorers, the next archaeologists, astronauts, hairdressers, chefs – the list is endless.

History has taught us so many valuable lessons and I have no doubt that these lessons will continue for years and years after we have hung up our mortarboards.

Children are taught in the same classroom, taught the same subjects and achieve well (for the most part), regardless of gender.

Conclusions

Gender divides have been ever-present in our society, and this section has served as a background to the rest of the book that will follow. By undertaking the research that I have to write this section, I have realised just how far society has come – and how far we have to go.

It's really interesting to see how much has changed over time, and how those changes have been made more and more rapidly as time has moved on. If this were to continue, then surely we should have completely free and equal societies in no time.

This chapter has explored how the Ancient Greeks had some brilliant minds leading the world with their views on gender and equality. Some female children in Ancient Greece were trained in combat, with the belief that strong girls made for strong women to carry children. The Romans believed that girls could be educated up to the age of 11 or 12, the usual age for a girl to then be married off and continue her life as a wife. Boys continued schooling until 14, which isn't a huge amount of difference. When we then shoot forward to Medieval Britain, gender gaps are openly regarded as natural, with women seen as fundamentally inferior to their male counterparts. Schooling for girls was relatively unheard of unless the child was from a wealthy background. It was feared that educating girls could be the beginning of them not wanting to fulfil their wifely duties. The beliefs of the Tudors that came after were not too dissimilar. With a country bound by religion, it was thought that girls should only be educated about religion, and that boys should be taught by a matronly woman from a young age – with leaders believing that hormones could take over and that studies would suffer at the hands of a 'marriable' teacher. For women and men in the Georgian period, appearance was everything. A girl with an education was seen by some to be unmarriable, and a boy who did not learn well and go out confidently into society was inferior to others. Boys were sent to boarding schools, women were uneducated, and the lower classes didn't really get a look in. The Victorians made some decent steps forward in the way of gender equality in education, with schools being open for girls, who followed a different curriculum to that of the boys. Here, girls were trained in the art of the home. Boys were subject to vigorous and sometimes unpleasant teaching methods that ensured that they left school with a great amount of discipline and also the skills needed to woo a lady. While Britain was fighting overseas in the world wars, some real changes were made to education, with the introduction of secondary schools. Secondary schools meant that education didn't end at primary, and that boys and girls could be taught the same subjects, to an extent, up to this level. After this, the different gendered curricula split quite obviously, with the purpose of girls' education being to make a successful housewife. It wasn't until after the war that society started to see the value that an educated girl could bring. With the advent of several educational reforms, such as the national curriculum, schools were mixed by gender and the biggest divides that were seen were based on one's wealth, rather than one's gender.

A brief history of gender education serves to underpin the development of the rest of the book. Knowing the long history that precedes the issues that we face now is crucial to understanding where we are in the process. Freeing education from gender bias took over 2000 years. That's an enormous amount of time for one half of the population to be treated as inferior in intellectual terms. If we look at the problems that are facing our young people today, we are still having trouble with some people arguing that there should be clear divides between the genders. Is this something that has been ingrained in us from 2000 years ago? Or are we generating new problems, new reasons that there should be divides?

How many of us discuss the gender divides that once were apparent in the classrooms that you teach in now? Or how those very divides narrowed and closed to form schooling as we see it today? I know that before I delved into the rich history of gender inequality, I hadn't broached the subject with my Year 6s because it didn't really enter my head. The children that we have in our care may not be seeing the same gender gaps in their education that existed throughout history, but that isn't to say that they are no longer there. Now I will definitely be exploring this element of history with the pupils in my class, who deserve to know how their ancestors strived to change things – and that it actually worked. Admittedly, it took a while, but they made change happen over those many generations, with just a few people speaking out about what they think is right. What a fantastic opportunity to show our students that change can be made, and that it is okay to speak out about it, because one day it might happen – and the sooner that it does, the better.

I currently work in a Victorian school. It was built in 1901, just before the end of Queen Victoria's reign. I did some digging around in the costume cupboard of my school not too long ago and there are still some sure signs of history around the old room. There are solid wood desks, names carved in with the year next to them. There are old song sheets and maths textbooks that take a really good wipe to get the dust off. Most interestingly for me, there was an old set of trays right in the corner of the room. My old archaeology head reared itself and I couldn't resist setting down the WWII jackets I'd discovered to take a little peek. I pulled out the trays and there were clear divides evident in the trays. Sewing needles – boxes and boxes of sewing needles that had been there for over 50 years. Sewing needles that maybe my grandmother had used at the school. Sewing needles that would have been placed in the hands of young women just starting out in their education. Sewing needles that would consolidate the future to which they were bound by history. This shocked me. I knew that there had been divides, of course, but to have them sitting in a room upstairs just brought home how little time had passed in history since these were used. I sat down with them in my hand, and rather than feel upset about the inequalities faced by so many women in our history, I felt overcome with pride knowing that women had fought for my right to receive the education that I have had. Women fought for me to sit in that room – with my degree and my postgraduate – even while holding those sewing needles in their young hands.

It may seem extreme that just by holding up some sewing needles I had this profound revelation of just how far we've come, but it truly humbled me, and it made me realise that we are incredibly lucky to be where we are now. If I can take one thing out of this life, it's that I want someone 60 years in the future to pick up this book and laugh at how we still have inequality in our day. I would love for them to feel like I did that day, holding the symbol of years of gender inequality in education, and understand that people wanted change – and fought for change.

1. How do you focus on gender gaps throughout history when teaching your subject to children?

_____

_____

_____

_____

2. What elements of the gender gap in history would you deem appropriate to teach the children?

_____

_____

_____

_____

3. Thinking back to your own education, how was the gender gap approached in your school?

_____

_____

_____

_____

4. How do you think your outlook may have been different had you been taught about gender gaps in your schooling? Do you think that would have changed way you teach now?

_____

_____

_____

_____

Section 2: Academic differences in children

Some of these headlines will be very familiar to you: 'Girls outperform boys at English'; 'Boys wear skirts in uniform protest over school's policy'; or 'Boys should not cry and girls should not get angry'.

Once a year, the entire population is subjected to examination performance and gender headlines. We are so conditioned, we analyse how one gender performs better than the other in various contexts and then ask why and what we can do to improve. By making this comparison, aren't we suggesting that boys or girls are not going to meet the same standard as their peers?

'The existence of such gender-emotion stereotypes is now well recognised', writes Claire Brechet (2013), designed to examine gender-emotion stereotypes in school-aged children. Brechet's research suggests that children conform to gender-emotion stereotypes when judging other people's emotions.

Could it be that children learn academic stereotypes from us in every pocket of society?

As Hollie explains in this section, it's not just a teacher's responsibility; it's up to everyone to challenge gender bias. One of the first classroom strategies a teacher could use is being thoughtful about their choice of language with all students and how this may be adopted by both genders and interpreted, or how a conversation may be adapted to suit the gender a teacher is working with.

Brief overview: boys prefer maths; girls prefer English

Gender in terms of education is a boiling pot for statistics! The higher powers just love having a gander at how boys are falling behind girls in their studies, while not offering any substantial ideas to help support change. Rather than seeing the same results year on year, this chapter will help you to implement simple strategies that have maximum effect both in the classroom and beyond!

Academic differences in children have been reported in national statistics since the introduction of the national curriculum in 1988. This has led to a huge focus on the fact that there are gaps between male and female children and results of testing. Teachers now have preconceived ideas as to how children will achieve based on whether they are male or female. In my opinion, it shouldn't matter whether a child is male or female. The child will achieve if they have the right guidance and if there are no extenuating circumstances which would hinder their achievement.

I am not going to make out that I believe that there aren't gaps because there are. What we need to explore is the why. Why are our boys 'underperforming'? What is it about our current system that makes boys less inclined to engage in the curriculum? Is there something that we can do as teachers to make sure the boys are achieving just as well as girls? In order to make boys more successful in our education system, I believe that instead of measuring how well they're doing using data, we should be looking at how we can change our curriculum to make sure that it is accessible for all.

While I think that it is common for teachers to despise data, I rather enjoy looking at it. Maths was never one of my strong points but I've developed an interest in data since I became a teacher. I think that it's really important that teachers don't just use data as a way to measure the children's attainment. Data should be used to interpret where there are gaps in the children's knowledge and I think a lot of schools are starting to do that now. In Wales, teachers have now started using diagnostic testing which allows teachers to see where there may be gaps. While this is a good step forward, some schools are still using this to assess how well the teacher has performed rather than using it to decide what needs to be taught for the child to reach the next stage of the learning. In England, teachers have moved away from using levels and have replaced them with stages of development. Again, this is better but I think that there needs to be something less summative to assess children. We hit a bump in the road when we complete these summative and formative assessments and segregate the results into genders. By doing this, by putting a separate column for boys and girls into our spreadsheets, we are encouraging a gap that doesn't need to be there. While the children are unaware of the fact that we do it, we are aware. It's almost like we have now been conditioned to believe that one gender is not going to complete their studies to the same standard as the other.

When we are faced with this in our data, we can be quick to make excuses for the reasons that boys have not achieved as highly as girls. What we should be looking at is how we can improve the data for the boys.

I once read a tweet from a teacher that stated that primary schools should be held accountable for 'gendering' children. And that's just what this is. Without thought, we are building social constructs for children without their input. We are inadvertently asking children, assuming that they will do so willingly and without question, to conform to a society that sets out the 'norm'. My question is, why should it be primary schools that are held accountable? Primary schools have the great fortune of meeting children very young, nurturing their minds, nurturing their emotions and building a very close relationship with them until they're 11 years old. While this would appear to confirm that primary schools should be 'held accountable', the baton gets passed on afterwards. It's not a primary responsibility. It's everyone's responsibility. For us to truly alleviate the gendering of children, we need to work together, rather than blame each other for apparent failings. No one is perfect, but we can be pretty close.

In this chapter, we will explore the differences in gender and attainment shown by statistics published in 2017.

Once all of the data is out the way, I will explore some of the myths which are prevalent in our schools and attempt to bust them, exposing them as nothing more than the farce that they are! As I've said before, teachers have preconceived ideas about pupils based on their genders, whether this is a conscious process or not. This chapter will serve to prove how unhelpful and unnecessary these ideas can be.

After dispelling these myths, we'll take a look at what the children had to say about the differences between genders in schools. I spoke with children aged from 3 to 18 to get a feel for what they believed to be the cause of divides – and whether they were aware of them in the first place! These discussions opened my eyes to how the children perceive their own differences and humbled me. I suddenly felt very fortunate to have been able to gather their thoughts on the subject. It made me realise that this book really is about them.

Possibly most importantly, this section covers delivery of classroom strategies. All teachers need strategies to complete their jobs. All strategies that will be mentioned are simple to put into place and even simpler to keep up with: small changes that can be made with minimal effort, but with maximum output for the child.

Statistics on gender gaps and commentary

This chapter will look at various statements made by the government on the 2017 results of national tests in England. I will explain the meaning of the data and offer some insight into how this might be combated in the future.

The gender gap at the expected standard in reading, writing and mathematics remains at 8% (as in 2016).

When looking at this statement, 8% jumps out as being quite the gap. Compared with girls, 8% fewer boys are reaching the required standard. When they are receiving exactly the same level of education, there must be some underlying issue. Are we failing the male members of our classrooms? Are we pushing the female members harder? These are natural thoughts to have as an educator, taking the blame onto ourselves because this is the one thing that we have total power over.

To break this down into actual numbers, 65% of girls reached the expected standard compared to 57% of boys. (Even without the gender gap, 65% is not a high proportion of pupils meeting standards.)

The fact of the matter is that it's not exclusively a teaching problem, it's an attitude problem from teachers and pupils. The difference between boys and girls is not down to ability, it's down to effort and a willingness to engage.

What's more upsetting is that this figure of 8% has been a constant since 2016. Yes, only two years – it doesn't seem like an awful lot – but what it means is that while we haven't slipped in progress, we haven't made any improvement. It's not entirely on us, but we need to be the catalysts for change here, making a conscious effort to bridge that gender gap.

The biggest gender gap in terms of single assessment units is in writing, where girls outperform boys by 12%; the smallest gap is in mathematics (1%).

The above seems to demonstrate that there is a massive gulf in the standards of boys and girls when it comes to writing. When we are giving writing tasks to the children in our class, are we ensuring that each individual child has a strong understanding of the importance of it? It seems to me that the boys in our classrooms are feeling limited, or perhaps even bored by the topics that we are putting in front of them.

How, then, can we make a conscious effort to supply them with something that we know that they will interact well with?

Simple idea #1: make the lesson interactive. Go outside, explore nature. If you can, get hold of some virtual reality headsets. Allow the children to explore different terrains – either physically or virtually – and write about them in detail.

Clearly, there is something in mathematics that the boys in our schools are able to interact with on a more positive level than they do with literacy. The thing that jumps out and screams at me is that in maths, there is logic, there is always a right answer.

In your lessons, create a problem for them in a writing task. I find that using Mantle of the Expert really is a surefire way of ensuring that the boys don't feel like they are writing simply for the sake of writing. Mantle of the Expert is a teaching tool that was developed by Dorothy Heathcote in the 1980s. It's since developed and is becoming a staple in many classrooms. Mantle is 'learning through imagination', where a teacher creates a fictional problem wherein the children act as experts in order to solve the problem, with the added pressure from a client who is waiting to see the final product.

At the higher score, girls outperform boys in all subjects except in mathematics, where boys outperform girls by 3%.

When we are talking about the 'higher score', we are talking about the children who are performing above the national average for age. This means that these are the children who have the best natural ability, and usually need the biggest push aside from those below national standard.

Again, we see that the pp is flipped in mathematics: boys tend to be stronger at the subject. What needs to be encouraged at the higher level is a **desire** to achieve more. A **desire** to be the best that they can be. To be classed as one of the 'elite' should be enough to make students feel more passionate about their education, but unfortunately this isn't what happens.

So how do we push those high achievers to give a damn?

Simple idea #2: set wide-open tasks. Set something out on the table with no instruction – a building project or a load of materials. Have some ideas in mind of what skills you would like them to cover but get them to explore what they can do with what you've given. Teach them to plan, teach them to think, to organise, to explore, to play. All students will have an inquisitive side; some just need a bit more coaxing than others. With this, you need to ensure that your pupils are engaged with the task, rather than seeing it as a way to mess around. You'll be able to tell the difference, just by knowing your class. Obviously, with boys liking something with a clear answer, this doesn't quite fit into what their ideal task would be. But given the interactivity of the task, all students should be enthralled with the materials, and in my experience, they find the answers that they need to through exploration; there's no requirement for this answer to be textbook correct.

This goes for both genders; we want to have consistently high standards, and this doesn't mean forgetting about the girls in maths or the boys in every other subject. It means finding your niche at planning activities that will provoke even the most stubborn of brilliant young minds.

Possible reasons for academic statistical differences

Looking at these differences has inspired me to explain why these results might be there. Undoubtedly, whichever issue is affecting your students, achievement deficits can be fixed – and you're the person to do that.

Attitude

Attitude seems to jump out at me the most. As our students get older, they all have their own changes going on. Hormones are developing and these can have a real effect on their attitude to learning. Gaps in academic achievement in the Foundation Stage are far less than those at Key Stage 4. From what I've seen, students' enthusiasm for education decreases dramatically as they move up through the system. They gradually have far more interesting things to be doing with their time, which is understandable – you're allowed to do a lot more when you're older!

As teachers, we need to think about how these attitudes can be turned back towards education. Exploring new avenues for piquing closed interests is the key to restarting the sparks that were once there for learning. If you have them hooked, there will be a considerable rise in academic achievement, let alone the bridge being built between the genders.

As students grow up, learning becomes way less 'cool'. I know from experience that I was a 'nerd' because I really liked doing well at school. I loved reading, and at the weekend I could often be seen doing a crossword puzzle. I tried not to be affected by people being negative but it wasn't always easy. If you can see this in some of your students, make them understand that it doesn't matter what anyone else thinks.

Stereotypes

Boys tend to subscribe to stereotypes more easily than girls. Stereotypes are rife in all walks of life. People expecting you to conform to different ways of acting dependent on what you might be: black, white, Asian, Hispanic, male, female, non-binary, effeminate, butch – and the list doesn't end there. Sly looks, questioning glances and innocent questions are the least harmful of the possible reactions to someone acting out of their 'norm'; but not all reactions are that minimal.

As adults, we have learnt to challenge what people might say – or at least ignore them. For our students, these stereotypes feel like the safest option for a person who, at this stage in their life, is just desperate to fit in.

For girls, stereotypes seem to involve wearing make-up, dressing in a particular way and engaging in gossip based on what we see in society. Fortunately, this doesn't seem to have too much of an effect on their academic performance but it can make them a little less willing to engage.

For boys, the stereotypes seem to be a little more detrimental to their academic achievements. Stereotypes associated with boys tend to be a lack of motivation, a great interest in sports and little showing of emotion. These are already visibly more detrimental to the learning process, because not only are boys having to compete with raging hormones, but they are also contesting against boys their own age.

Due to these stereotypes, boys – and girls, to a lesser extent – seem to become less interested in their academics, which I think may have a large role in why the gender gaps are so high in secondary education. It's just not seen as 'in' to be the one that isn't engaged in the social etiquette of acting to their gender.

Social development

As our students move on through their education, they build relationships. In primary school, children build super-close relationships with both their teachers and their peers – partly because they are constantly in such close proximity with each other. This is an amazing process to watch and it's one of my favourite parts of being a teacher in the primary sector.

As students move up to secondary, they are suddenly faced with brand new people, with brand new ideas and different ways of doing things. They have different teachers for different subjects, which is all incredibly exciting – and that in itself is a huge credit to the secondary sector.

Where we begin to see more academic gaps between genders, we also see students segregate themselves from other genders because relationships formed as we get older mean something different from the childhood relationships that we were used to. Mixed-sex groups lessen and students distance themselves from other genders, not wanting to be seen as fraternising with the dark sides. In primary school, children have no hormones that are telling them that boys and girls can't play together. In secondary, we see girls and boys who hang around with the opposite sex being branded with unsavoury labels.

Relationships don't just change with other students. With so many different teachers, building a relationship is a lot harder than it is in the primary sector. We teachers find that we are just seen as people who are trying to stop the students from enjoying their new-found freedom. We become the enemy rather than the confidant; the authority rather than the consoler. In secondary, this becomes a more evident problem. Children fight back against the people that they deem to be trying to dominate them and this can lead to resentment and a lack of engagement.

Build relationships with all of your pupils. Make them understand that they are helping to construct the gap between primary and secondary. Just because a student moves to secondary, it doesn't mean that the care isn't there. The baby gates have just been taken down a little bit.

All students go through a change in high school, and this is in part to do with them developing their social status. In terms of academics, children begin to resent the people that they once would have trusted due to issues that arise during puberty. This leads to children being less willing to engage in lessons, preferring to be building their social status among their peers.

Closeness to end of compulsory schooling

Another factor that can and will affect a child's academic performance is how close they are to being able to make a decision about furthering their education. As students move up through schools, they are closer to making that decision, therefore there may be a dip in how much they are willing to participate. I liken it to taking part in PE lessons. You try different sports as you move through school because it's compulsory for you to do so. Then, in Year 9, you suddenly have the freedom to choose whether you want to do PE as a GCSE. If you choose not to, you undoubtedly put less effort in, because you don't believe it'll benefit you.

Getting our students to engage when this is the case can be a real trial. When someone knows that they are not going to have to do something in a short while, it's difficult then to build up the motivation.

The differences between genders may be noticed here more with subjects such as art becoming much more interesting to girls and PE for boys – this is not the case for every student but appears to be for the majority. These subjects are more vocational than the core subjects, and therefore the students are more likely to want to fill their time with something that they have chosen to take, rather than something that they are required to. As we reach the end of the school year, dips can be noted from most children, they are no longer as engaged – and given that testing periods come at the end of the year, this isn't a great time for that dip!

Ensure that your class don't take the dip by creating innovative and interactive lessons that still fulfil your need to teach the skills, keep rigorous methods for behaviour management and create nice, physical activities that have them hooked.

Myth-busting

Myths and legends are common in all human cultures and narrative traditions. **We have no difficulty in seeing the unlikeliness of the dragons of England and Wales battling for dominance or the incredible powers of the wizard Merlin. However, when it comes to myths that we encounter in schools, we take them as gospel.**

For years, educators have had predispositions ingrained in them to believe the academic differences in boys and girls are 'just one of those things'. They're not! And by feeding and responding to these fallacies, we only further their reign and add fuel to the fire for gender inequality.

All of the myths stated here I have heard first hand from educators; and the purpose of this section is to provoke thought, rather than confirm scientific falsity!

Myth #1: 'Boys have a limited imagination.'

Now this myth I've heard echoed by countless educators. I have an issue with this on two levels.

Firstly, imagination will only thrive when given stimulation – as with most things. If the boys in your school or class are lacking in imagination, the best place you could start to improve this would be your own practice. As teachers, it's our job to nurture minds into believing that they can do more. That way, their minds will also believe that they can do more, work harder, think bigger.

Secondly, not only are you reaffirming something with no hard evidence, but you are also using it as an excuse for the poor performance of boys! But if we're expecting from the start that the boys are not going to do as well as the girls, it's not surprising that we're not really doing anything to change it. But you can change it. As teachers, we have a huge responsibility to make children believe that anything is possible. How can boys have limited imagination when that is our superpower as teachers? Don't limit them and they'll show you what they can do.

Sure-fire ways to spark boys' imaginations!

1) **Get them reading.** Something that they won't be able to put down. All teachers remember one book that changed their life – be the person that ignites that fuse with them by finding the perfect book.

2) **Use their interests**. If they enjoy Lego or *Minecraft*, get them creating their own worlds! Allow them to conjure up utopias or dystopias; let them explore whatever terrain their mind deems exciting.

3) **Make it physical**. Re-enact a famous battle on the field, explore mountains on the climbing apparatus, echo the weather using musical instruments. By creating these worlds in your classroom, you are opening their minds to see what they haven't before. It's still imagination, except you're helping to construct the initial idea, like planting a seed for a tree.

Myth #2: 'The child will respond differently to a teacher because of their gender.'

There seems to be a culture in schools wherein 'naughty' boys get sent to male teachers for discipline. I mean, come on! Speaking from experience, I remember fearing one teacher the most from my school days and she was the tiniest woman I ever met! This myth is believed by so many teachers and it needs to be addressed. As a female teacher, I see no difference between myself and my male colleagues. I'm no more or less equipped to deal with behaviour from either gender, I am no more or less adept at furthering the progress of either gender, and I am no more or less able to form a relationship with either gender. Moreover, it can't be nice that just because someone is a man, they have to (not always but more often than not) conform to society's expectation of a man: to have to be the disciplinarian to children who would probably benefit from forming a relationship with an adult – any adult – who is trustworthy to them. It just doesn't seem fair. As teachers, it is super important that we form relationships with all of our pupils. Unfortunately, sometimes we can slip into the gap of only building a rapport with the people that are our own gender because, in theory, we have more in common. As adults, we don't only have friends of one gender. So why does it happen in our schools? Children will respond to you if you show them that you care. It can be really easy to conform to this myth without thinking so here are some questions that you can ask yourself from time to time.

Thinking points:

1) How many non-school related conversations do I strike up with pupils of my own gender?

2) What about with the opposite gender?

3) Could I do more to build relationships with other genders?

4) How?

Number 4 is key – because if the answers to the above made you think, you need to explore how to make a change in your classroom.

Myth #3: 'Girls are better suited to creative subjects such as the arts.'

Given that I have a background in theatre, this myth really grinds my gears. I class my gender as nothing more than a drop in the ocean when it comes to creativity. My gender has no influence on the effort that I put in when acting and I can firmly say that it has no impact whatsoever on my ability. I class myself as a fairly creative person, but no more than my male counterparts!

In our classrooms, we all have pupils who are less fond of creative subjects such as the arts. This tends to stem from the fear of embarrassment in front of a crowd rather than lack of interest due to gender. Some of the best performances I have ever seen have been given by males. That's not to say that the arts that you do in your classroom should be Tony Award-worthy; however, if children are willing to participate, then this should be recognised! I once had a child in my class who would come close to tears every time that there was a mention of a presentation or a performance. It made me uncomfortable that he was feeling that sad. I would never force a child to perform in a drama lesson if they didn't want to; however, I saw this child as a challenge that I believed I could overcome. I sat down with him and we talked about why there was such an incessant fear in him and he opened up to me and explained that he didn't feel like he would be able to speak when called upon in front of people. So, step-by-step, we started to broaden his horizons. I would ask him direct questions in class that would require more than a one-word answer and while there was a stutter sometimes, he gained a lot of confidence. We reached a point where he signed up to the drama club that I run in school and auditioned. I class this as one of my triumphs as a teacher – not for me, but for him, because I feel like I helped him make a difference in his life.

I believe that this myth is absolute rubbish. The arts are a way to express yourself, regardless of your gender, and to put a limit on who should be able to participate is just nonsensical. Instead of avoiding creative subjects such as dance with boys, try looking at them from all of the perspectives that help the child.

Benefits of creative subjects

1) They help to build confidence in areas that children may struggle in, such as how they look or how they think that they are perceived by others.

2) They allow for difficult subjects to be discussed without having the pressure of a 'serious' lesson, e.g. drink-driving (secondary), familial issues (primary).

3) They can provide a platform for free speech – something that lots of our children miss out on in our education system.

Being classed as a boy or a girl doesn't even begin to come into it.

Myth #4: 'The curriculum is too rigid to meet the interests of boys.'

Let me just float a theory in front of you.

People might not be so keen to put their all into something if it isn't made appealing to them.

Pretty out there, maybe.

I can unequivocally say that if something has the opportunity to be tailored to me but isn't, I would probably not want to participate in it. As children, our students have no power to make decisions such as curriculum change. Therefore, it's no real surprise that we find ourselves with reluctant learners.

The theory that the curriculum doesn't support the needs or interests of boys, in my opinion, isn't true. The reason that it isn't true is that anything can appeal to whomever you want it to, if you make the effort. I would say that we are quite lucky to have the opportunities to have a little bit of leeway in the way that we teach what is on our curriculum. That is the one thing that the curriculum doesn't prescribe.

Where we fall down is assuming that boys and girls have specific interests. If we are going by the common aspirations of *hairdresser* or *footballer* then I believe it is fair to say that not all boys like football, and not all girls like hairdressing. I have tried to understand the other side – how the curriculum may be tailored more to boys – but to no avail. Where curriculum is prescriptive, it's not exclusive. Or at least it doesn't have to be.

My ideal solution lies in the teachers' ability to manipulate the curriculum to the needs of the child. Well you have a curriculum, you have children and they have needs. Why are we still relying on a document that has not and will not change drastically for a long time? Make the curriculum your own – make it appeal to the boys who we are always focusing on; make it meet their interests.

Three steps to success for meeting boys' interests

1) **Know their interests.** No one can create a bespoke product when you don't know what your client needs. Find out a common interest that your male students have; it might be that male and female students in the same class all share similar interests. For example, children in my class love collecting football cards.

2) **Explore opportunities.** Look at the curriculum with your class in mind. There will, no doubt, be skills that need covering that could be done in a different way to support the interests that you found out about in Step 1. With the cards, they are full of data – that definitely ticks off some skills in the national curriculum!

3) **Measure the success.** Try out lessons using the opportunities that you have discovered. Rely on a little assessment for learning to establish what your students felt about the lesson. Of course, looking at the work completed is important from an academic perspective; but if the interest is there, the skills can be developed because you've got them like a fish on a hook. For my class, I would come up with a lesson that would enable me to teach them how to analyse data using a subject that many of them enjoy.

Myth #5: 'Boys and girls learn according to different theories of learning.'

To say this is a gender issue goes against any logic that we use as teachers. No one has the exact same way of learning as anyone else. I know that the theory of learning that I work best with differs from that of my best friend, my partner and my colleagues. This is part of why our job can be so demanding; catering for different learning preferences coupled with varied learning abilities makes differentiation paramount to successful teaching. It shouldn't be a matter of 'how boys learn' and 'how girls learn'; treat them as individuals, not as a group.

All teachers understand the three principal learning theories and successful educators will ensure that they juxtapose a mix of all three to create the best chance of progress for the students. While some boys and girls may learn differently, this is no variant to the fact that some individuals learn differently. Just carry on doing your job, ensuring that every child in your class has their learning needs addressed!

Let's recap the three theories of learning:

- Behaviourism: children learn through rote, discipline and structure;
- Constructivism: children learn through independent exploration;
- Social constructivism: children learn through the 'zone of proximal learning' wherein they learn alternative ways of thinking from their peers.

So, in order to ensure that these three styles are addressed, let's look at four tips for ensuring that no one is left behind.

How to create a learning environment for everyone

1) **Use all three styles.** Like I said before, educators should be using a blend of all three established learning styles for their children to progress well. Sticking to one is ignoring the fact that some children may not work to the best of their capability because it doesn't suit them.

2) **Ask the children how they think they work best.** This comes back to building relationships with the students that you teach. If someone asked you what your perfect learning environment was, you would appreciate the thought. They know what works best for them.

3) **Assess where <u>you</u> think the child learns best.** Still keep your own eye on whether the student may work better in a different capacity. If this is the case, then ensure that the student has a choice in the matter – we don't want to create a reluctant learner!

4) **Give ample opportunity for change.** As with all humans, students may well change while in your care. They mature, become more independent and discover more about themselves. Don't limit your students to one learning style. Let them explore and they might just surprise you!

Myth #6: 'Only boys learn well in competitive learning environments.'

I have yet to meet a child who doesn't love getting one up on their peers. Yes, some students would rather avoid the pressure of competition, but in my experience, they are few and far between. A little healthy competition in the classroom increases focus and boosts progress. Boys may indeed enjoy a competitive learning environment; and they may benefit academically. But girls are no different. By making this segregation, we are adding to the crevasse that is separating our classrooms into genders. Plan activities in your class with the thought that all of the children are going to benefit.

I love using competition in my class. I also love partaking in these competitions too. I am quite childish in that I will not let the children win at anything! This is one of my most valuable tools. If the children win all the time, they are nowhere near as invested; whereas when they feel like they could really achieve something by 'beating the teacher', they can't wait!

When we are looking at gender, it's so important to ensure that you are not assuming that the stereotypes we have are the same for every child. Some children may feel uncomfortable with the confrontation that can come with competition, so as the facilitator, try to put down some ground rules explaining that any animosity will cause the activity to end – we don't want any overzealous competitors as this would ruin the point!

Some ideas to boost healthy competition

1) **You vs them**. As I mentioned before, I love joining in with competitions and my pupils love any chance to beat me! This allows them to be competitive but as a group. They have to work together to take down a single person and there is something truly gratifying about this. Something that I have used as a starter activity for maths is a times table grid where we have a leaderboard on the wall. We time ourselves for how long it takes to complete, and I take part too! I always win (so far, at least!), but that just gives a bit more competition for the higher achievers.

2) **Class vs the world.** So that it's not always you being trashed, try a competition that includes some higher power. I find that using an activity such as 'Name all of the countries in Europe' at the end of a lesson can consolidate knowledge about certain subjects and create a great competitive environment where you enter as a team and win as a team.

3) **Silent competitions.** A pub-quiz-style competition can be a great competitive activity – and it can be even better for those who are less fond of competition by making it silent. Children can only communicate by writing on whiteboards and showing their teammates.

4) **Outdoor learning.** Take the competition outside using a trail. Set up clues around your school and have the students answer questions on different topics to set them on a real-life treasure hunt! The competitive attitude is then more spread out and it supports collaborative learning.

Myth #7: 'Single-sex classes would alleviate gender gaps.'

Single-sex classes are a thing of the past for state schools in the UK and to address this myth, we need to ask why the separation of sexes was abolished. Debates are still ongoing as to the benefits of mixed sex classes and it's worth exploring. People in favour of mixed-sex education argue that the children become more well-rounded by associating with the opposite sex. The other side of this argument is that having opposite-sex students in the same school is a cause for distraction.

If it was the case that having single-sex classes would alleviate gender gaps, surely the issue lies in the teaching of different sexes, rather than the ability of male or female students. If it is being suggested that boys underperform because they are distracted by the girls in the class, I'm not sure I would feel very happy with this assumption if I identified as a male! Surely this is an insult to the academic prowess of the male student!

I believe that if the teacher is able to provide appropriate stimulation for the learning, then the other members of the class should not be the main focal point of the classroom.

In my opinion, single-sex classes would be a huge step backwards in the fight for gender equality. Also, it might raise the question of the gender of the teacher, which should not be a problem.

Some questions to consider

1) **How could we explore the possible benefits of a single-sex class?** Is there a way in your school that you could try single-sex classes for a limited amount of time to complete some first-hand research?

2) **Are the gender gaps in your class more visible with a higher percentage of either sex?** All teachers know whether they have a 'boy-heavy' or 'girl-heavy' class, so look at your data. Say you have a 70% female class; are the gaps more visible than they would be with the opposite being the case? Does it reflect the percentages of gender that you have in your class?

3) **Where would we teach the children who associate more with the social constructs of the gender opposite their biological sex?** While it's a contentious subject for some, there are children in our care who are more inclined to associate with the gender that doesn't reflect their sex. It is important to think about how the segregation would serve these students and what long-term effects this may have on them.

Myth #8: 'Boys prefer non-fiction reading.'

Every educator has met students that just don't like reading. I am a firm believer that everyone can be a reader; they just haven't found the right book. It's a cliché, I appreciate that, but I honestly believe it! And I take great pleasure in introducing a child to a book that sparks a lifelong love of reading.

Boys, in my experience, do tend to be more reluctant on the whole, but this is not to say that they only enjoy non-fiction. There are so many incredible pieces of literature that should appeal to both genders. Books that make you think – and feel, and explore, and challenge – should be part of an ever-growing repertoire of learning.

This is not to say that non-fiction books have no benefit. Of course they do. Students are entitled to favour whatever kind of literature that they want to, but as teachers, we can and should try to ensure that we give children the most depth and breadth of reading that we can offer.

I have always been an avid reader. I was raised by a family who loved books and my personal library consisted of a range of reading materials, both fiction and non-fiction. I have therefore made it my mission as an educator to pass my love for reading on to all of the students that I meet.

My favourite fiction ideas for reluctant readers of any gender

Key Stage 2

- *Wonder* by R J Palacio: a beautiful read about acceptance and how we are not all the same.

- *The Giver* by Lois Lowry: a thought-provoking book about a dystopian world where all colours and emotions are taken away.

- *Harry Potter* by J K Rowling: a magical saga about a young boy who discovers that he is a wizard.

- *A Series of Unfortunate Events* by Lemony Snicket: a series of books about three resourceful children who are pursued by an evil villain after the loss of their parents.

Secondary

- *The Curious Incident of the Dog in the Night-Time* by Mark Haddon: a book about how a young person with autism deals with love and loss.

- *The Hunger Games* by Suzanne Collins: a trilogy based on a dystopian future where young people are elected to fight to the death for entertainment.

- *Noughts & Crosses* by Malorie Blackman: a story about a society where black people are above white people in terms of social status. Interesting read to understand injustice.

Myth #9: 'Girls and boys are naturally different and that's why they learn differently.'

Nice little debate to end on!

Now, this gem has caused no end of discussion with anyone that I have brought it up with. There are two sides to this argument.

Side one: Boys are naturally born stronger. Their bodies are more capable of dealing with matters of physical strength and less equipped to deal with emotion. Girls are naturally disposed to have a more maternal instinct and this is inherited genetically.

Side two: Some women are much stronger than some men, and heavy-duty jobs are not simply ignored if there are no men, but rather the woman takes on the role themselves so this is not exclusive. Some women do not feel a desire or need to have children and can feel drawn away from children and the thought of ever having one.

Do we simply behave in a certain way because that is what society dictates to us given our gender? Or are the roles that we find ourselves in determined by nature in our genetics?

It's definitely interesting to consider the different sides and whether the theory that we are biologically different to the extent that we should be treated differently has any legs. When it comes to the students we are educating, are we equipping them to believe one of these arguments, both or neither? I believe that children should be asked to explore the differences between people who associate with being male or female and what this means for them in terms of academics. Aside from teaching them that it's okay to be different, we are also teaching respect for both genders. However, we do need to be careful that we are not falling into the trap of making either gender believe that they are limited by this.

It's important that we think about these things when wanting to bridge the gender gap in our education system.

Gap-bridging questions to consider

1) Have you approached the subjects of biological differences and gender differences with your children?

2) Could some of your students possibly feel more in tune with another gender than the one commonly associated with their biological sex?

3) Does the fact that a male student in your class finds childcare or cooking interesting, or that a girl enjoys engineering and mechanics, mean that they are 'unnatural'?

Hopefully, these points have given you some food for thought, and whether or not you agree with my opinions on them, you can still enter your next debate with plenty of varied theories!

Conversations with teachers from all phases

Nick Hodges: primary classroom teacher, Year 5

How do you cope with building relationships with the female members of your class?

I believe it is important to build relationships with all members of my class, regardless of gender. At the beginning of the year, I provide activities and opportunities for dialogue to gain an understanding of their interests, hobbies and personalities. By doing this, it not only aids the personalisation of my teaching, but it helps develop and build relationships with my pupils.

What are the main differences that you notice between boys and girls in your class?

There are not many clear differences between the boys and girls within my class. I have noticed a common ground of interests, especially when it comes to games and technology. The boys and girls interact well with one another and friendship groups are generally mixed gender. To pinpoint some differences, as a generalisation, the girls can behave more maturely in some cases. The majority tend to ignore undesirable behaviour whereas some boys tend to get involved. However, boys can show more resilience to small disappointments such as not being able to play the games they want to – or with who they want to – during playtimes. In terms of academics, there is a female-heavy interest and attainment in narrative writing. However, I have seen an increase in boys' interest of fictional reading over recent years.

Are there any strategies that you use to overcome any gender barriers?

I believe attitudes towards gender can be a barrier in themselves. It is often heard, 'I need two strong boys to help me,' which does not send the correct message to children. Statements like that can define a purpose for both genders, which is far from the truth.

For a number of years, I have held the position of being the only male teacher within my school. I have never seen this as a positive or a negative. It is often said that it is a positive to have a good male role model in a school environment; but I have always had the opinion that any good role model is vital, regardless of gender. As the only male, I have been asked in the past to deal with the 'naughty boys'. This sends out the wrong message. It is very similar to the old saying of 'Wait 'til I tell your dad.' All this does is diminish the authority of a female.

As a role model to impressionable children, I believe it is vital for all adults to choose words wisely and to change our own attitudes towards gender or we run the risk of developing the next generation with aspirations, self-belief and attitudes determined by their gender.

From working across phases, do you notice any differences or parallels between Foundation Phase and Key Stage 2?

The main difference, in my experience, has to be the pupils' attitude towards gender. I'm not sure whether this is ingrained in some pupils from a very young age where toys or games are very gender-orientated or whether it is something we as educators have not addressed.

As a Foundation Phase teacher, I remember one day, I came to school wearing a pink tie (I thought it was fashionable), but I didn't expect the response I got from the pupils. Pupils in my class and pupils from others' classes, just walking down the corridor, all commented on it. 'Why are you wearing a pink tie? That's a girl colour.' I didn't realise it would be so controversial. I know when I have worn the same tie, as a Key Stage 2 teacher, and it didn't cause such a fuss. This got me thinking about the world our pupils live in and the information that is presented to them in order for them to form their own opinions about everything. If you walk into any toyshop, it is clear to see where the boys' and girls' toys are located. There is a visual divide with the pictures of boys and girls on the toys – and also a divide in the nature

71

of the toys. Girls appear to have the options of toys to teach them how to care for a baby or cook and clean, whereas boys have the options of tools to fix things, diggers and cars. There is a clear divide from a very early age. It teaches them what jobs they should do and what they should be interested in. Sorry, I went on a bit of a rant then!

I have also noticed some similarities in my experience across phases. Compared to girls, boys tend to achieve lower standards in literacy attainment. Our school and national data proves this across both key stages. Digging a little deeper, boys struggle to show flair when writing narratives. I would suggest that boys in the Foundation Phase would be more interested in reading a non-fiction book over a storybook. The advice given to parents and teachers suggests that children need to be exposed to good storybooks from an early age to ensure good progress in their writing. If boys are uninterested in fiction reading, they are more likely to be uninterested in fiction writing. As a school, we have tried to address this by purchasing storybooks to engage the boys – with mixed results.

Having attending a course on the matter, I have also used games to inspire writing. It was advertised specifically to raise standards in boys' writing; however, I found amazing results from all pupils. I used a game called *Myst III: Exile*. It is an immersive, adventurous game revolving around different worlds and an engaging, self-paced storyline. It immediately aroused the pupils interest. I created short tasks to develop descriptive writing, predictions of what will happen next and letter-writing. It was a fantastic tool to use and the impact could easily be measured.

What is your top tip for ensuring that boys and girls achieve similar standards?

Treat all pupils as individuals, regardless of gender. Engage learning using their interests and use many different teaching methods to find the key to unlock their love for learning. Not every method will suit all of your pupils, so use a variety. I find that pupils only learn when they want to, so make them want to learn.

Debbie Eccles: headteacher

As a headteacher, what would you say are the main differences between boys and girls at primary age?

In terms of behaviour, I think that from nursery, girls seem much more prepared for school in general. Boys tend to be frustrated far more easily; it almost seems like they're more primal, with animal-like tendencies to want their own territory. Then at about Year 4, boys seem to think that they need to become more macho. Genders separate into their groups and develop the 'pack' mentality throughout the juniors. Then in Year 6, girls and boys tend to gravitate back towards each other and they mix better than other ages. I'd say that the emotional development is slower between the ages of 3–8 for boys, and this gives a visible gap between boys and girls.

In terms of academics, the biggest difference that I see is again that emotional development. Our data for 2017 showed a 28% variation between boys and girls at the higher levels in Foundation Phase, with girls storming ahead of the boys in Personal and Social Development. In general, at Key Stage 2 the biggest difference that we have is in reading. Boys fall short of the mark at higher and standard levels.

Do you think that the differences in boys and girls mean that we treat them differently?

Yes, I think we do. With boys playing rough on the playground, we are more likely to turn a bit of a blind eye than we would if it were girls scrapping. I have seen this in all schools that I have worked in; it just seems to be one of those things. With girls, I think that we tend to be more sensitive towards them and more accommodating to their emotional needs because they show more emotion than the boys. Boys close down or get angry or frustrated. It's not something I have ever really thought about, but I suppose that we do treat them differently.

Are there pressures for you to minimise the academic differences in children?

Yes, from a national level. The national agenda in Wales is for us to close the gap between boys and girls in literacy. However, they haven't offered any suggestions on how we can help to do this. What frustrates me is that while we are required to raise the standards of literacy for boys, we don't have any push to ensure that the girls are exceeding also. It feels almost like we are slowing down to speed the boys up. What there should be is a push for girls in maths and science. If the gaps are so big in literacy, why aren't they seen as big in other core subjects? There should be an equal push in those too.

A more personal directive that we have had from our challenge advisor is to bridge the gap between boys and girls in PSD at Foundation Phase. We were told to provide opportunities for boys to display the emotional behaviours at the higher level. We are already trying to do this, of course, but a 28% gap is massive. There has to be an underlying issue there.

How much responsibility do you think schools should take for ensuring that children see genders as equal?

We as a school do have a huge amount of responsibility. We have to guide the pupils. Currently, we do this by providing opportunities for the children to see positive role models and by giving equal opportunities to all genders. We think it's hugely important for us to instil a sense of confidence in all pupils. I think that we have a staffing issue, having only one permanent male teacher and two male teaching assistants. Our children see females as the more nurturing gender, and this isn't always the case; but by the amount of female staff members that we have, it's not hard to see where the children get this from.

What are you doing already to bridge the gender gap and promote equality?

We have a very fair uniform policy. All students are able to wear trousers or skirts if they wish to do so. So long as the uniform is tidy, we don't discriminate. We have also tried to get more male role models in school. For example, we are inviting male parents into school for an open day. We want the children to see that men can be just as nurturing as women. I do believe that there is a natural difference between boys and girls, and I think that we are predisposed by our genetic makeup.

Rhiannon Kelly: secondary maths teacher

Given that you are a maths teacher, how enthusiastic are your students to partake in lessons?

I think it depends on age. You have Years 7, 8 and 9 who are really enthusiastic to try new things. I wouldn't say that they are eager to partake in traditional maths lessons of textbooks and questions. But even so, if you relate it to something that they're interested in like physics, or the world or modern day, you get a bit of enthusiasm. But with Year 10 and 11, they don't really like trying new things. They seem to be fixed on the idea that they just answer the questions because they're programmed to do these exams. They're no longer fresh from primary where you studied one topic and did everything related to that topic. When I did my placement in primary on my PGCE, the topic was 'volcanoes' so everything was related to that, science and maths. The teachers have to get really creative. Year 9, if you catch them, they love it because it feels like primary but is higher level and they love it. Years 10 and 11 have the pressure of GCSEs coming up. They know how important it is and it turns them off. They know if they don't get this and that then they'll never be a doctor or whatever. It depends on age, I think.

Following on from that, then, do you notice a difference in genders?

Yes, massively. Boys talk the talk: they want to be an engineer, they want this and want that. So, you give them advice on that and yet nothing changes in class. Girls do the work but they don't talk it up – 'Oh, I don't know if I'll get a B' – and it drives me mad because they have more capability than the boys who big it up. Girls put themselves under so much pressure and it doesn't come out in the tests. I think their lack of confidence hinders their ability to perform because they struggle with it. Some girls are confident and know that they can do it – I was one of them! I would definitely say that boys are more focused on what they want to do. Girls don't seem to aim as high. I'm not sure whether that's a societal thing.

Would you say that there is a biological difference between boys and girls?

No, not in terms of ability. There are differences in students but I have seen boys who really struggle with maths and girls who succeed exceptionally well in maths. I can't see the difference. I think it's more of a conditioning difference, the way that they are raised, the way that they are presented in society, and about confidence. Girls don't have the confidence but they have the academics. They tend to be quieter, putting their heads down. Boys are more easily distracted, they mature later – which they do. Students are students.

As they move up through school, have you noticed the attitude of lower-ability students change?

I have only been teaching for two years so it's difficult to say. But I have seen low-ability students tend to start to give up. For boys, it's like 'Well, who cares?' They may be masking something. But for girls, it's more of a stress. Because they mature quicker, they're thinking about what they want to do in the future. Boys won't even bother to try and look past tomorrow. And I think it's a fear of failure for the both. If you've been in lower sets through school then you're used to it. They say to me, 'Oh, we are the thicko class,' and I feel awful because that's not how they should be feeling. As soon as they believe that, they feel the same thing. But the genders deal with it differently.

Where do you think that the lack of confidence stems from in girls?

I can't see where it stems from. I don't think that they are pushed as much. They're not exposed to things that my daughter is now. She's 7 and she has been exposed to all different toys like Lego, building sets etc.; whereas the girls in Year 10 and Year 11 had dolls growing up. They didn't have the push of 'You can do this, and you can do that.' It was more, 'You can have nice eyebrows.' I think they're kind of conditioned to think – well it's not, it's a subconscious thing. Some of them think that they're just a girl so that's that; but some don't and then they push and they're not happy that they don't see the results that they want. I know as a woman that I compare myself so much to other people. Society paints us a picture of the woman who has it all. The woman who has an amazing figure, amazing eyebrows and a perfect made-up face and brains, and a high-flying job, and children and a gorgeous husband. These are the characters that we see all around us: one-dimensional women. So when we're not getting those things, we feel like a failure rather than looking at our own achievements.

Have you noticed any parallels between a child's home life and their ability in school?

Hugely. I think it's the attitude of the parents. Especially in my last school where the kids were like, 'Well, my mum never got any qualifications and she's alright,' and 'Those bloody teachers, you don't need university.' They're always told what they don't need, rather than what they can do. So if you're coming from a third-generation family of non-workers, you don't see the escape. I think, especially dependent on the area, we expose these children to things that they have never seen.

I took some of mine on a trip and they had never seen a sheep before. And they were 12/13. If you've never left your estate, except to go as far as the shop, how can you ever see yourself past that? Even with all the technology that we push their way, they still only get exposed to what they want to be exposed to. Now I'm in a school the other way round, where parents are really high achieving; students tell me about how much they're being pushed. The parents are telling them what they need to do. This provides problems of its own in that children feel this massive pressure bearing down on them, having a breakdown if they get a B instead of an A. Their horizons are so different.

How do you provide for different genders in the classroom?

Well, I mix them together – I love doing that. I try to pair low-ability boys and girls together and the same for higher ability. You have to take advantage of their hormones too. Placing a pretty, outgoing girl with a shy lad who sometimes shows off, the boy will be much quieter because he wants to impress the girl usually! In terms of activity work, I have to keep the boys busy. They have to be busy from the moment that they come in the room. Girls can come in having a full conversation and still have their stuff out ready for the lesson. Whereas with boys, I have to be at the door ready and giving them repeated instructions. It sometimes feels like I'm teaching in primary, which I'm not. I use treasure hunts, relays, anything to make sure that the boys' minds and hands are occupied. It means that they get involved with things without actually feeling like they're getting involved. I have to ensure that lessons are broken up. For a girl-heavy class, I find that I can give a task that they will sit and complete in silence for 30 minutes; whereas in a boy-heavy class, I have to work in short bursts, it has to be punchy. Otherwise, they get distracted. I think that it's a maturity thing. My Year 11s are boy-heavy and I've had to come up with a completely different plan for them. I need to get their motivation up to get a B, even though they already have a C. I struggle to bring boys back to the lesson if it's not quick activities; girls are no problem.

Can you think of one top tip for smashing down gender barriers?

Don't make it an issue. Everyone should be the same. Ask them all 'Don't you want to be a pilot?', 'Don't you want to be an engineer?', 'Who here wants to be an architect?' There's no difference.

However, as a woman, I do try to lift up the girls and I give them space to answer. The boys are more confident to put their hands up so I make a conscious effort to make the girls aware that I want them to respond too. At the same time, you don't want to embarrass a shy boy because he wants to be a dancer, or because he is gay. You don't want to make it an issue in your class; you want to make it an issue in your planning. As a teacher, you need to be aware of possible issues in the classrooms. It's not a rare occurrence where a confident pupil will make a passive comment that can be offensive. Rather than screaming students down for saying something that could be deemed as sexist, you almost minimise the significance of what they are saying, showing that it doesn't matter to you, hopefully deterring them from doing it again. It's no fun for them if they don't get a reaction. I'm seeing that that is the way to go. It's just allowing them to voice their concerns if they need to, without trivialising it.

Julie Walker: primary classroom teacher, Year 1

What seems to be the biggest difference between boys and girls in Year 1?

Well, most of them do still come into school with quite a fixed idea of who they are, what they can wear, what they should be, how they need to behave in a certain sort of way. For example, the boys seem to think that they are programmed to be boisterous outside; the girls seem to think they should always be small, neat, at a table colouring. And that's what they do! Nobody has said anything in school to them but in Year 1, they behave like that kind of automatically.

So do you think that may be ingrained at home?

I really don't know, because you see children who have no little brothers or sisters and parents are sometimes – you know what their jobs are, and they're not 'stereotypical' jobs. But the children still come in and act like that. And then you see others with a big family, or mums who are – well, let's say hairdressers. (I know that's stereotypical but there are adults that do those sorts of jobs.) And when you talk to them and hear stories, they understand that they can be what they want. We teach growth mindset so they are aware that anything is possible if you reach for it. If they get stuck, they work things out, so they know that they can be or do anything. But still, if you do a page in your PSE book, you still do see those things. Girls, it's things like nurse, teacher, hairdresser or work in a shop; and boys are policeman, footballer, a rockstar. You see those sorts of things without doing or saying anything to promote that really.

In terms of academics, what are the trends that you notice at the end of the key stage?

Erm, when you look at the data, each year people try to say 'Ooh, there's the trend, there's the pattern: it's up 2%; it's down 2%,' but those percentages are just different children each year so we try and teach in a way that it limits the damage, if you like. We teach maths- and science-type subjects in a way that it will appeal to the girls, where they can use things to help their understanding. Same with boys: we choose topics that will help them. So, we do construction – building the Taj Mahal and things like that – which will engage boys, but in a 'girl-friendly' literacy-type way. So the figures at the end of the key stage: I don't think they really show up anything particularly, not huge gaps at age 7.

So, do you think that boys tend to be more interested in science-based subjects?

No, and they don't see themselves as 'boy scientists'. We've had two trips recently to do with science and in them, we were all just scientists.

There was no 'Oh, I'll be the one that writes that down, or puts the coat on.' They were all the same thing. Sometimes we are all artists, or explorers. We try not to make that anything that has gender as a barrier.

How do you find forming relationships with the different genders in your class?

I think that because we do the One Page Profiles at the start of the year, it helps set the scene because there are some quieter children that you wouldn't know, unless you did that sort of activity, what they would like. I have one boy who is in *Thomas the Tank* land all the year around; he's going to work there when he grows up so he has very fixed ideas about what he likes and what he wants to do. But there are quieter children, and if you didn't do that activity then you probably wouldn't know what they like because they don't stand up and say, 'Oh, Mrs Walker, when we do construction, could I build a castle because I really want to be a prince when I'm older.' You know, they don't do that sort of thing.

I think, personally, because I have two sons, you almost have a sort of background already. I know that times change and that fads come and go; but generally, because I used to tap into their interests when they were little – learning their interests and finding where they wanted to go – it's a little bit easier. Being female, the relationships with the female side are almost more naturally already there. So, I don't really know if it makes a huge difference, for me it is easier if you have boys at home and you're a girl.

How do you cope with any gender issues that arise in your class?

Well they are keen to talk about things, which is what you want, isn't it? You don't want them to just think things and not have the opportunity to ask questions and find out who thinks what and why, what makes you think that and who says you're right. Of course we want that discussion, but it'd be done in a calm way so that everyone could have their turn so it's appropriately pleasant in the classroom. I'm hoping that by keeping it calm, they would all feel as though they have had the opportunity to share and be heard but overall, they would all come to the understanding that we are all different, we all have strengths. Just because you haven't had a chance to play rugby yet, it doesn't mean that you can't be a great rugby player for Wales's women's team when you're older. It might just be that you haven't had that opportunity yet or might not know that it exists for you to do. That's the message that I would want to get across really.

What is your top tip for ensuring that there are no gender barriers in your classroom?

We try to deliberately provide resources that are open ended. So, we don't have a dolls' house, we don't have a car garage, we don't have those sort of gender stereotypical things to play with. We have blocks so you could build a house or a car garage, but we don't put in anyone's mind that there are limits to this toy, so it's a girl toy or a boy toy. So, when we look through the catalogue for what to put into class, that's something that most people now do. When we are talking about role play and when the children have their child-initiated learning, we try to steer them into something that is equally accessible for boys and girls. We have a hut outside that can easily be transformed into a cottage for the girls to play ironing or make the tea for when dad gets home; but we try and use it as a building, so at the moment it's a bakery, everyone is having a fair go because bakers are boys and girls. Next term when we switch to the Great Fire of London, it'll probably be Samuel Pepys's house where the servants will be men and women equally and they will all be taking turns in rescuing each other from the fire. So the ideas are bigger than the characters and the roles that they would have within it. They are the two main tips: role play and resources.

Mark Hanson: secondary PE teacher

What is the biggest difference you notice between genders as a secondary PE co-ordinator?

The biggest difference comes at Key Stage 4. At this age there appears to be a change in what female pupils think towards the subject when it comes to value and the importance of the subject. Effort levels with females appear to drop and they are a lot more conscious about what their peers' view of them when it comes to sweating, red faces and what is expected from exercise. There is also a change in how competition is used in lessons. Males seem to thrive in general on competition whereas the female cohort do not appreciate it and would prefer to do an activity which takes away this element.

How might you combat the differences in school?

At school we offer a range of opportunities for female pupils to participate in single-sex classes when they have PE even when on the same timetable as the males. We offer opportunities to be physically active but take away the competition element of sport – for example: Zumba, dance and fitness.

How do you find building relationships with the female members of your classes?

This is pretty easy. As a teacher I feel it is vital in the job to build positive relationships with all pupils. As a result, I will do my utmost to learn about the pupils to help create an environment which they can learn in.

What is your top tip for ensuring that all genders are achieving similar standards?

Differentiation and excellent teaching. The department is lucky to have outstanding practitioners who can invigorate and promote our subject to pupils and this creates a safe learning environment for them to develop their skills. Make mistakes and learn.

Classroom strategies for bridging the academic gender gap

1. Be dramatic

'I just can't get the boys to engage in role play!'

Being dramatic in the classroom by encouraging male students to get up and involved with drama in a positive way increases confidence and self-esteem. Get out of the habit of accepting fate and encourage students to participate!

Some teachers may shudder and curl up at the thought of using drama in the classroom, but it's one of the most powerful tools a teacher can use. If you are confident teaching maths and science, then role play is no different. Drama serves as a way to confront otherwise-difficult situations in a more practical way!

Consider assigning a male member of the class as a female character – not as a 'dame' but as a powerful woman. They don't have to dress up or wear make-up but it's interesting to see how they act in someone else's shoes! Some of our students will have a lot going on outside of school and role play can be a great tool to let them get out of their own mind, even just for a short while.

Take my Year 6 class. We studied *Macbeth* last year and instead of asking one of my self-assured girls to play the part of Lady Macbeth, I asked a shy boy. This timid child stood at the front of the class and embodied what it was like to feel like Lady Macbeth, convincing her husband to commit atrocities. No one laughed; the rest of the class were in awe and that is the power that drama has in the classroom.

My three top tips for using role play to encourage the boys in your class!

1) **Don't let them rule the roost.** A strong level of discipline is necessary when using drama in the classroom. Ensure that they understand that this is still school, and the same rules apply. It's not a chance to mess around for half an hour.

2) **Don't be afraid.** So many educators are put off using role play for fear that they will make a fool of themselves. Remember that the pupils are taking their cues from you. If you show that it's okay to do it then they will soon follow.

3) **Explore different styles.** Research some drama games that can be helpful in role play. Students will always respond to a game, and while they are enjoying themselves, they will open up.

2. Degender your class

'I can see huge divides between the genders in my classroom'

Ensuring that your class know that there is no barrier in terms of gender in your classroom can mean that pupils can get along with their education without feeling like they are inferior or superior to other genders. By taking careful measures to ensure that no divides are visible, students will be happier to engage with the lesson.

We create divisions where they shouldn't be created. We sit our students 'boy, girl, boy, girl', reaffirming the belief that girls will gossip and boys will misbehave. Don't make an issue out of something that shouldn't be one! Seating plans are crucial in most classes but sitting boys next to girls, and vice versa, can sometimes cause them to feel negatively towards the other genders because they feel like it's something that they are being forced to do.

I would suggest that teachers stop using gender as a point for praise, like 'good girl' or 'clever lad'. It's not because of the pupil's gender that you are giving praise. Praise is a great tool but you need to be careful there is no segregation caused by giving it. Similarly, with discipline, be careful that you are being fair on both boys and girls. Often girls can get away with a lot more than boys in the classroom and this is noted by them – leading boys, especially, to believe that female teachers don't like them as much.

Seat students where you know they should be seated to gain the most understanding. If you have a full table of one gender, who cares? If you don't make a big deal out of it, then neither will they.

How do you know that your classroom has been 'degendered'?

1) There are no male- or female-specific posters or charts.

2) You strike up conversations with students of both genders, and build relationships with everyone that you teach.

3) Boys and girls in your class interact willingly and with respect.

4) There are no incidences of sexism within your class or around the school from your pupils.

5) There is a high level of collaboration and creativity from both genders.

3. Settle behaviour

'I just can't get the boys' behaviour sorted so they can make good progress!'

Trying to balance all of the plates that we handle as educators, behaviour issues are one of those 'tough to manage, even harder to maintain' jobs that we could do without. By ensuring that your behaviour management of all pupils is solid, you can relax in the knowledge that your class have enough respect for you to listen to your teaching.

It's ingrained in us to think that boys are less well behaved, when actually, if you communicate well with a 'difficult boy', they soon cease to be 'difficult' – but they are still stuck with the label 'boy'. The child may be male; however, this doesn't have any impact on the child's behaviour, no more than it does with what he likes for breakfast. Don't commit yourself to believing these archaic stereotypes. Treat each child as an individual, not a gender.

I would suggest that behaviour management often stems from the culture that you set up in your classroom. Some teachers have a strict classroom setting wherein even a breath out of line can have terrifying consequences; on the other hand, we find classrooms where perhaps the rules are a little too slack and children are allowed to rule the roost. It's only common sense that a balance of the two is the way to go to keep behaviour in check.

Understandably, all teachers want their class to make progress; that's one of the main reasons we put so much effort in. It's crucial that we don't let behavioural issues get in the way of the incredible teaching that we no doubt have in store.

Useful tips for settling behaviour that rarely fail

1) **Have some calm music playing quietly.** As the children are coming into your class, I'd advise that you didn't have Dua Lipa blaring out of the speakers; that's not the culture you want to be creating. Instead, play some acoustic versions of songs that they might be familiar with and turn the music down just enough so that they have to be silent working to hear it.

2) **Ensure that students know your boundaries.** From the first time you have the class, lay down your line. This is where it is, this is where it will stay. It's always better to be firmer and then soften because once they think they've sussed you, you're stuck like that for the year.

3) **Start lessons with a collaborative problem.** If the problems that are arising tend to be at the beginning of the lesson, have something on the board or the desks for them to get instantly involved in. Add a little competition to get them hooked. Children misbehave when they're not engaged.

4) **Ask them how their day was.** I've said this before. You need to build a relationship, it's one of the most important tools that we have. Take an interest in how they are today. If you know that a particular student can be challenging, don't have preconceptions about what they're going to be like.

4. Explore the modern world

'How can I inspire both genders to achieve through my teaching?'

All around us we have great role models for both genders. When we are teaching, we all think about what our students might aspire to be

in the future. I am almost certain that one pupil that I had will become Prime Minister – I've never met anyone with such drive, let alone at ten years old! So how can we ensure that our students also have the drive that we think they should have?

Take a moment to think about what we would class as an aspirational job. Are you thinking about male- or female-centric jobs? Or does this not come into it? In the next section, you will read conversations with pupils of all ages who have their own way of defining who particular jobs are right for.

In my class, I like to ask them to look at people like Theresa May and David Cameron and ask the children what the differences between them are. Does their gender define what they can and can't do? Some children may surprise you by not even entertaining the thought that they are different genders.

It's such a cliché that we think of certain jobs being for men and women but we all do it. Note the title of the book: you have an immediate picture in your mind. It may be subconscious, but it still finds its way in.

What I want to try to instil in the pupils is that their gender shouldn't deter them from doing something that they think they want to.

How to abolish gender from aspirations

1) **Give alternative examples.** When discussing people in a field of expertise, try to sometimes (not all the time) give an example of someone with a job that wouldn't ordinarily be seen in the role. For example, most people working in IT are male, so instead try to discuss a woman being a CEO of an IT company. It just broadens their horizons to know that the norm isn't a necessity.

2) **Show counter-stereotypical examples.** When studying specific topics, ensure that you include people who would oppose the norm too. A female footballer and a male hairdresser come from two respectable fields that are dominated by one gender. Do some research on different role models and you might be surprised by what comes up!

3) **Get them to explore their own options.** Back to the students: they will have some kind of idea what they are interested in. Talk to them and ask them what they want to do, if they could do anything. Exaggerate the point that they can achieve what they want to achieve, as long as they put their mind to it.

5. Change your mindset

'I just don't see the point in this; nothing is going to change.'

I get it. You're busy; you have more than this going on. But unless we make a change, the next generation – the generation that we are educating – are going to go through life just the same way that we have. Unequal pay, unequal opportunities, unequal treatment. It needs to stop somewhere – so let that point be you.

These strategies will not help you if you aren't fully invested in what they mean for your students. We want to create a world where our children don't feel burdened by their gender. As teachers, we need to understand the gravity of the responsibility we have when developing the minds of the next generation. By reading this book, it's already clear to you that something has got to give.

Given that we have grown up in a society where we are still judged on our gender, even in our personal lives, it's no wonder that our children are growing up the same. Subconsciously, even only in part, we still think like our parents did – just as they thought like their parents. Our views on gender are deep seated and it will take a conscious effort to usurp them.

My solution is to change your mindset. 'Growth mindset' is all the rage these days and rightly so! To encourage children to not give in, to try again and to thrive from small improvements – that's a super way of thinking. I remember from my own school days having a feeling of shame if I didn't get something right that I was struggling with! We need to take this mindset on and use it to benefit our students – and ourselves too!

Changing your mindset!

1) **Think outside the gender box.** When you're doing your extensive planning, try to think about the activities and how you've catered for each gender. Ensure that you are trying to boost male imagination and female intuition and logic.

2) **Explore your own demons.** Look at your own practice and how you relay things to the students. Do you have any preconceived ideas about genders coming into your class? If so, think how you can combat these. If a thought about a 'difficult' boy arises, banish the gender from the thought. Treat all children as equal.

3) **Allow for slips.** With these changes in your thought patterns, there are bound to be slips where you revert to praising genders or assuming results. If this happens, don't give up; just make a conscious effort to distinguish next time.

4) **Keep looking forward.** This is key. Once you think you have mastered the gender gap in terms of academics, keep looking for more opportunities to decrease the gap. Their education is in your hands, so do your best to make sure that they leave you with a strong feeling about who they are and what they are capable of.

These strategies should help to bridge the gender gap in your classroom. Looking at yourself is imperative as you strive for change. It stems from you. The students look up to you, respect you and listen to you – give them something worth listening to.

Conclusions

This section has hopefully enlightened you on how there are academic differences between genders in our students. While there are differences, what I wanted to achieve with writing this section is to explore how these differences should not deter us from treating each child as an individual rather than as a product of their gender – a mistake that is being made far too often.

When looking at the statistical differences between genders, we see that there are factors that are attached to these differences that aren't entirely academic. A huge shortfall in the differences between genders is their attitude to learning. As they progress through school, it's not a rare sight to notice that boys' attention and attitude decreases. Now, what teachers need to be asking is: why? There has to be a reason that boys are becoming more and more disengaged with their learning.

As teachers, ensuring the positive attitude of our students is often half the battle. Engaging boys in activities that stimulate their interests and promote progress should be second nature; learning shouldn't be something that is just expected to happen.

As they go through school, our students experience huge changes in themselves and in the world around them. They are heavily influenced by matters outside of the classroom and often they run the risk of being classed as 'uncool'. It's not cool to want to do well in school; it's cool to do what everyone else is doing. Academics take a back seat for most during their adolescence – they're far more occupied by more leisurely ventures. When we allow for this disengagement, accepting it as one of those things, we lose our passion, we lose our fire and we are not doing justice to the students in our care. It shouldn't matter that they don't want to learn. Give them lessons that are enriching, that are personalised and that are appropriate to their individual needs.

We looked at a variety of myths in this section that I had overheard in various situations. Teachers discussing pupils in the staff room, teachers talking to parents. I heard some at CPD events. We live and breathe our kids, so it's no surprise that they are at the top of our talking lists wherever we go. What these myths do is instil in us a sense of, 'Well that's just the way it is.' Rather than challenging ideas that we find wrong, we sit back and accept that other people who have more of a say will go on and change how we see gender in our classroom, when this shouldn't be the case. We all want the best for our students, so why are we letting misconceptions and idealistic views cloud our judgement in our own job? It's extremely rare that you will find two students that are the same, that have the same needs – let alone half of your class! Gender divides are generally around

50/50, so naturally, we tend to split those classrooms in half: boys and girls. What we often don't take into account is the fact that we are reinforcing the differences in these children when really, in education, gender doesn't actually come into it. In the past, when schools were dictated by the genders that existed within them, yes: gender mattered. But when we teach the same curriculum to every child who walks our corridors, why are we still separating them by society's expectations of how they should behave? Stop taking what other people say as gospel; make your own mind up about the differences between the students in your class.

In my interviews with the teachers for this section, I really wanted to get a scope of what teachers in different stages and levels thought about gender in their classrooms. I anticipated that there would be a big split between this for teachers and I wasn't wrong. When children are younger, they tend to have set ideas about what boys and girls can do and this tends to be influenced by the things around them such as television and their peers. As we move up through schooling, we are then confronted with students who are keen to abolish any kind of difference between genders. Key Stage 2 teachers were forthcoming with how they felt the differences in gender affected their classrooms, explaining that the differences in gender were only really apparent when looking at how mature a student was, with girls tending to mature quicker. When we move up to high school, we seem to revert back to the gender divides that split them when they are little. Teenagers are very affected by the world around them, and this means that they are constantly battling to fit in with what they class as normal. Studies take a back seat in favour of the need to blend. I picked interviews with maths and PE teachers because these are two areas, in particular, that see a big gender divide, and this came across during the interviews. Where girls are less confident in both subjects but capable, boys tend to appear more boisterous because this is how they are predisposed to behave – especially in sports. They, themselves, are reaffirming the behaviours that are appropriate to boys and girls because this is what they have grown up with. The issue lies where there is mistreatment of either gender because they don't fit in with the prescribed behaviours.

My view on this is that we tend to go on a merry-go-round with how students view themselves and their gender. At an early age, behaviours appropriate to their gender are ingrained in their mind. As they move to Key Stage 2, these differences become less apparent, they find common ground and friendship groups are usually mixed. When hormones are then thrown into the mix, our students drift further away from mixed groups, because the changes that have occurred for them mean that they are no longer similar to the children they were running around the playground with a few years ago. As educators, we need to try to shift these divides to be more like plateaus. All the way through schooling, it should be imbedded that children are children, regardless of what gender they may be.

While it is easy for me to rant about how there are many incorrectly perceived differences between the genders, it's no use without providing strategies for the classroom that are easily implemented and have great effects. The skills that it takes to put these strategies into your working life are next to nil; you just have to want to make a difference for the future of your students. So, don't teach to genders, do talk about the differences, explore how other great people have achieved while giving equal time to all genders.

Degendering your classroom has been met with criticism in the past from people who don't want to change something that works. Except it doesn't work. Gender inequality has no place in the 21st century and it is still causing issues with children growing up feeling affected by what they can and cannot do because they associate with a given gender. Be the teacher that makes gender a non-issue for your students.

1. How often does your school divide by gender? What for?

_____

_____

_____

_____

2. Do you feel that there is a need for this separation by gender? If so, what need does it fill?

_____

_____

_____

_____

3. Are there any other ways you could split the children for academic data? What ways?

_____

_____

_____

_____

4. Looking at information in this section, what changes would you make to your teaching?

_____

_____

_____

_____

5. What would happen if you stopped assessing data by gender?

_____

_____

_____

_____

Section 3: Aspirational differences in children

As Hollie argues in this section, 'not all boys like football, and not all girls like hairdressing'. How often have you steered a student to a subject or career choice? I suspect as a teacher, this may well apply to a large proportion of our conversations with children, particularly secondary teachers when dealing with subject choices and university.

One of the thousands of students I taught at school breaks all gender conventions. Jawahir Roble was 16 years old when I taught her GCSE Design Technology between 2008 and 2011. She would always arrive to the lesson overheated and full of energy.

At the time, the school population was predominantly Muslim and served the London Borough of Brent. With all the hallmarks of an inner-city school and the challenges this brings a school community, there was a strong belief amongst parents that the boys' and girls' schools ought to be separated, even though they shared the same site! At the time of writing, the community's wish did not match the multi-academy trust's financial plans. Just two years later, both genders began to work and play under the roof of the same building.

Many years before the school amalgamation, as a school leader supporting school life in the playground, I would enjoy watching Jawahir play football. On some occasions, she would join in with the boys from the sixth form. Her passion for sport was clearly nurtured by the PE teachers and a small group of students who played in the football team. I took pleasure in attending some of the football matches and leading the team on some rare occasions.

Seeing that she is a Somali female who grew up with eight siblings in North West London, many would assume Jawahir's future was largely predetermined by her gender, perhaps her skin colour and also her religion. It is heartwarming to see Jawahir break all conventions and receive national recognition!

'Who would ever think a black, Somali-born immigrant girl with eight siblings could ref a men's game in England with a hijab on?' (Olley, 2017), Jawahir said in an interview with the *Evening Standard* newspaper. In 2017, she became the coach of the first-ever Football Beyond Borders women's football team and reached her level 6 refereeing qualification.

She 'currently earns around £35 per game – £20–£25 if officiating as a referee's assistant'. I wonder how this compares to male referees at the same level 6 qualification?

Jawahir represents millions of students – boys and girls – who can break convention. If only we all actively challenged our preconceptions.

Off the field and back in the classroom, I am reminded of a story which tests our biases. I attended a school assembly during the last academic year and a teacher addressed the students while the parents gathered in the school hall:

'If your mums are not in the audience, they have either not yet arrived or they will be coming tomorrow. Don't worry!'

As a father, I immediately felt ostracised. As a school leader, I wondered about any of the children gathered who may (just) have fathers at home, any looked-after children and children with foster parents – those who do not know who their mothers are. It was a subconscious slip of the tongue, but let's imagine for a moment how a young person may perceive this simple comment and inadvertently be made to feel different.

Ask yourself: are you conscious of the advice you give to a student? Is this gender-focused? I suspect subconsciously it could be. Next time a student asks for your advice, make a conscious effort to reflect on what advice you give, regardless of gender.

Brief overview: the blueprint of life

I heard someone talk once about the fact that we have a 'blueprint of life': the idea that from birth, we all have a path laid out for us. Not laid out by anything out of the ordinary; just by society. It's the idea that we are already on the path that society wants us to take from the moment we first take a breath.

It's a daunting thought, but it's true. Society has an ideal plan for us all, and if we deviate from that plan, it either pays off or it doesn't. We are conditioned into believing that we need to learn to walk, to talk, to read, to write, to pass exams, to go to further education, to find a job, to work, to retire, to die. And every single person goes through these steps in one way or another. Those who break from their predetermined path are those that society has a certain view of, positive or negative. By persistently following these paths that are set by the environment around us, we are slowly reinventing the wheel over and over again.

This isn't a book on philosophy (although that would be an interesting read!) but it is about the paths that we take, and the paths that we subsequently lead the students we teach down. Our students look to us from the age of 3 to guide them along their path so that they can carry on with a bit more awareness of what is going on around them. What we (and society) tend to do to our students is teach them that they have limits that are already laid out. Everyone knows the phrase, 'Don't stray from the path' – well why not? There may well be an exciting world out there that we are too stuck in our ways to venture into.

As adults, we are very quick to stop children exploring for fear of them getting hurt or making a wrong decision. How are they ever going to learn whether something is a good choice or not if you don't let them make mistakes? Children take in everything around them, even after they leave education. In this blueprint of life, shouldn't we be mapping out a little less stringently so that our students have a right to make an extension?

Children and families come in all shapes and sizes. Some come from deprived backgrounds and some from affluent. Both of those and everything in between helps to shape the future of the students in your classroom. Some will grow up with limited experiences of the world, meaning that they probably won't want to go out and explore, much preferring to settle down into a job just like the generations of family that came before them. Some will have an abundance of opportunity thrust at them from a young age. These children may go on to be doctors or scientists, but they also might not. The environment that we build around these children is like a body of water, with children being the sponge.

Ideas about gender roles are heavily formed around what our students take in, both at home and in school. Gender roles are taken from parents, family, teachers, religious figures. Everyone around them helps to build on a once-limited picture of the world. If we limit that picture to certain stereotypes of people, that child is moving forward in the world at an immediate disadvantage. Tolerance and acceptance need to be taught; aspiration and determination need to be taught. Without those, we are leading the blind until we can't lead them anymore.

It is no secret that the workplace for adults is not an equal environment. It is all over the media that women are speaking out for fair opportunities and equal pay. Two thousand years after the Ancient Greeks, we are still not living in an equal society, but being duped into thinking that we are. No one knows about the differences until someone makes a stand. It shouldn't have to come to that in the forward-thinking culture that we claim to have. It shouldn't take someone reaching the end of their tether after realising that they're being treated unfairly for something to change. This section will explore the ways in which we can cement a more equal, less gender-biased future for the blueprint of our students.

This section will move away from the conventions of academic achievement in children to look more specifically at the differences in aspiration in our pupils. Academics are not the centre of the universe as children may think in youth, but instead they are the foundation, the building blocks which allow the children to grow and learn until they reach their capacity – which should never be with us.

The majority of this section will be made up of conversations that I had with children. These children range from age 3 up to 18. I conducted them first-hand because I find that this is one of the best ways to find out what's going on in people's heads. Communication – who'd have thunk it!

We will look at the differing views of the children and why their experiences and views may be so different from one another. This will form the basis of the subsequent areas of this section wherein I will again look at some myths in order to debunk and offer suggestions as to why they're even around in the first place. This will be followed by ideas of classroom strategies, using real examples of tried and tested lessons that help to raise the aspirations of your class to where they can't be raised anymore, realistically.

The series of conversations that I had with these students was the most eye-opening thing I've ever done. They were open and honest, and that allowed me to really delve into the psyche of the child that I have sitting in my classroom every day – and the child you have sitting in yours. I laughed at some responses to questions and cringed at others, but every single response has gone into this book verbatim. The children have a right to be heard, so I have to give them a chance to speak.

I conducted lots and lots of interviews with children and students of all ages. These interviews had unbiased and open questions and each of them has been transcribed verbatim. The purpose of conducting these interviews was to see how children viewed gender at different ages and when the changes occur most obviously.

Conversations with students

Year 1 – Seth and Eve

Who is better: boys or girls?

Seth: I think boys because boys, like, in my class Kion is really speedy.

Eve: Oh, I don't know because I think boys and girls both have loads of different talents and the same talents, like I'm speedy too.

What is your favourite toy at home?

Eve: Oh, I know, I have a toy tiger called Herman – I cannot get to sleep without him. I don't really play with him though because I'm usually at school or I go out places.

Seth: I have this dog called Chatty Charlie. He's my best dog ever.

Do you think that boys can wear pink?

Seth: Yeah! My dad likes pink.

Eve: It's my uncle's favourite colour!

Seth: Boys and girls can wear any colour.

Eve: Someone in my class says that only boys can like orange, but orange is my favourite colour! Some people – boys and girls – don't like colours because of their football team. My dad hates red.

When you're bigger, what do you want to do?

Eve: I would love to be a singer. Or I would be a vet, nurse or a dancer.

Seth: I would be a dog trainer. I am fond of dogs.

Do you think that boys can be nurses, dancers and singers?

Seth: And they can be actors.

Eve: They can be any job. Except if they're jobs for girls.

What jobs are just for girls?

Eve: Well, I'm not sure but I don't know about ballet because you never see a boy doing ballet.

Seth: My sister really likes dogs, so she could be a dog trainer. I think they can be anyone. They can be a police, or a helicopter driver or a firefighter.

Eve: I think they should just follow their heart and be what they want to be.

What do boys like doing?

Eve: I think they might like football.

How about girls?

Seth: I think girls like doing ballet, tap dancing, singing, acting and maybe dog training. Basically, they can do anything.

How do we know, when we are little, what boys and girls are supposed to do?

Eve: I think that you learn from making mistakes.

Who do you play with more – boys or girls?

Eve: I play with mostly girls. I actually like a boy in our class.

Seth: I play with boys, I even have friends who are boys at church. I'm friends with boys because I am a boy.

Analysis

Year 1 had their own ideas about genders and these were pure and simple. The children understood that there were differences between the genders but did not believe that this should affect whether they can and can't do things. When asked about their favourite toys, neither child chose a toy that is stereotypically more associated with a specific gender. So, this raises the question, is there a need for gendered toys? The children were very clear about what they could do as they grow up. Their options were not limited by the fact that they saw themselves as a boy or a girl, and saying 'they should just follow their heart and be what they want to be' shows a wisdom beyond their 5–6 years.

Year 3 – Zac, Josh, Libby and Harmony

Firstly, do you have an opinion on whether boys or girls are better?

Zac: Um, boys. Because we know more about science and football.

Josh: I would think, um, both of them because it's not good if one was better than the other because they're both the same. They're both good at jobs.

Libby: No, because I think they're both the same because first: that's fair; and second: just because we have different things doesn't mean we are different people.

Harmony: That we are both as clever as each other, no one is better. Because it wouldn't be fair.

What would you like to be when you're older?

Libby: Policewoman. It's just like a really interesting job. Not a lot of people that I know want to be something like that. You need to be brave, um, strong.

Josh: I would want to be 24 jobs. I want to be an ice hockey player the most. I don't watch it but I do watch *Dancing on Ice*. I can't ice skate but I am learning. I've only been once but I'm looking forward to when I'm older when I'm doing the 24 jobs. I'll probably have to go to university before I start all them jobs. I would learn different things in university and when there was no learning on, I would go to ice hockey places.

Zac: I want to be a scientist because you get to invent new things and you get paid more. You need to be brave because you don't know what will happen as soon as you make something. Also, you need to go through school, college and university and if there's anything afterwards, I don't know about that.

Harmony: I wanted to be a singer and someone that dances on ice on the show Dancing on Ice. I've only watched it once but I really loved it.

Are there any jobs that only boys can do?

Libby: No. One word, that's it.

Zac: I don't think girls are very good at being in the woods.

Josh: I don't agree. My opinion is that one job is not really good for girls. Ice hockey player. Sometimes, girls when they have skates on can go too fast and smash into the wall and really hurt themselves.

Harmony: Only boys can be gardeners or farmers. I've never seen any girls who are gardeners or farmers.

Libby: My friend's mum was actually a farmer in her old job.

Are there any jobs that only girls can do?

Harmony: I don't think that a boy could be a ballerina. It's quite graceful.

Libby: Same answer as before. No.

Josh: I think that boys aren't allowed to do hairdressing but a barber's is different. I had one at the hairdresser's but I would prefer them to be girls because most of them are girls.

Zac: Nope. Boys can do anything girls can do.

Does being a boy or a girl mean that you're better at certain things in school?

Josh: No because they still have a life. No matter what they do, they still have beauty inside them.

Anything else you would like to add?

Josh: Only thing is that boys and girls are different because most men have short hair and some have long hair, most girls have long hair but some have short.

Harmony: They look different, they like different things and come from different places. Girls like to wear makeup and boys never wear makeup.

Libby: Like popstars, just because they're famous, doesn't mean there's something special about them. They're just normal people but they just sing for us and stuff.

Zac: I would say that girls don't like sewers. Girls don't like getting dirty; they always wanna shower afterwards.

Libby: I actually went on a farm once and there was sheep and sheep poo everywhere. I stepped in it and when I got home I was like, 'Ugh, get me in a shower.'

Analysis

At 7–8 years old, these children definitely had their own views on what they thought about gender, and these views were split depending on their gender. The boys, Josh and Zac, had clear ideas as to what they thought that boys and girls could do. Hearing them talk about how they thought that girls don't like to get dirty, and that girls couldn't play ice hockey, was entertaining when watching the female children's reactions to their comments – which were in no way malicious. I had a real mix of children within this group, and they didn't let other people's opinions differ from their own. The children in Year 3 did feel that there was a difference between the genders and how they are supposed to behave, and this is a common feeling for them to have. The aspirations of the children were, for the most part, quite stereotypical, with the exception of Libby who thought that her wish of being a policewoman meant that she had to be strong and brave – not your stereotypical characteristics of a woman. Libby provided the conversation with her view on injustices that she felt. She was quick to respond to anyone saying anything that would suggest that either gender was superior over the other.

Year 4 – Jessica, Maisy, Lincoln and Rio

Girls or boys – which are better?

Jessica: Boys. I think it's because I'm more of a tomboy than a girly girl.

Maisy: I think boys are better because I'm a tomboy as well, and because they play all these games, and not dress-up games like girls.

Lincoln: And, loads of boys have actually entered the Olympics.

Rio: Boys because they play more sports, they're more fitter and they can do more stuff.

If you could be one thing when you're older, what would you be?

Maisy: An electrician. My dad is an electrician and I just like to see all the stuff that he does with wires.

Lincoln: I would be a taxi driver. Just to start off with then I'll probably get another job.

Rio: A footballer – for Man United.

Jessica: A teacher for primary school.

Thinking of those jobs, could other genders do them?

Jessica: Yeah, boys can be teachers at any age.

Lincoln: I've seen a lot of boy drivers, and a lot of girl drivers.

Maisy: If you're a tomboy and don't mind getting dirty then you can be an electrician.

Rio: You can do both because some girls might like football, and they have teams.

Are there any jobs that you don't think a certain gender can do at all?

Jessica: Be a fairy princess entertainer at a party.

Lincoln: I was just thinking then of jobs and then I was like, no I've seen boys do it. Like a nurse, but my actual granddad used to be a nurse. Or a woman entertainer but boys can dress up as girls. I think actually, you don't see many girls being a builder. Most girls like clean things, and builders get covered in cement.

Who is the best role model you know?

Maisy: My cousin because she is a kind person and she would do anything for anyone.

Lincoln: Mum and Dad, because my mum gave birth to me.

Rio: My friends because they always stick up for me, and they're kind to me. They play with me.

Jessica: Peter Bunzl, a person who writes the books I like.

Are you friends with more girls or boys?

Maisy: Mixed, because I think it's nice to have different. I have one best friend who's a girl, and one best friend who's a boy.

Lincoln: I kind of have a mix, but I mostly play with the boys because I'm that gender.

Rio: Mixed because there's some people in this class that I actually know, so I play with them. Most of them are boys though, because they play good games.

Jessica: I play with the boys because I usually act more like a boy than a girl.

Where do you think we get our ideas about how different genders should behave?

Jessica: Most people in the council think that boys should be boys and girls should be girls. Boys have to be into boy stuff, usually have short hair and wear boys' clothes. Girls usually wear dresses, have long hair and high heels.

Lincoln: Say like, I'm a boy, my dad says you should wear this, and my mum tells my sister what to wear.

Maisy: You see all these people walking around and you see boys playing football and boys think, oh I should do that. Then you see girls like dressing up and it's the same.

If someone said something mean to you about what you want to do in the future, what would you say?

Maisy: Just because we are a different gender, doesn't mean that we can't do something.

Jessica: Just because we are girls, doesn't mean that we can't do jobs that boys do.

Lincoln: We can do whatever we want in life.

Rio: It's our life, our choice. So, if we wanna do girl stuff, we can; and if a girl wants to do boy stuff then they can.

Analysis

With Year 4, I was surprised with the conversation leading to the fact that all four children thought that boys were better as a gender. Both girls in the group classed themselves as tomboys, meaning that they found themselves to associate with traits that are usually attributed to boys. What was lovely was the fact that there was no issue with them coming forward and saying this; what was surprising was that they felt they had to explain themselves as to why they felt they had gone against their own gender. With their future aspirations, this group gave a wide range of jobs that they wanted to do and were quite simply bemused when I asked them if the other gender could do the job – this just wasn't something that had entered their minds when picking out their future self. Something that sparked in my mind was Jessica telling me that the government are to blame for our ideas of how boys and girls should behave. It's so ingrained in them that they behave differently, and Jessica's explanation for this was that it was because of a higher power, rather than something in their control.

Year 5 – Jess, Ollie, Eleri, Tyreese

Do you think it matters whether you're a boy or girl?

Jess: I don't think it does because, you know, it doesn't really matter, we're all the same kind…

Ollie: It doesn't matter because there's only small differences but they don't affect how people would do stuff.

Eleri: It doesn't really matter because say if you were a boy who wanted to be like a girl, and people were laughing at you or something, you can be who you want to be. Not be ashamed of who you are.

Tyreese: Like Ollie said, it doesn't affect like, what you can do.

Do you think there are some subjects that boys are better at? Or girls are better at?

Ollie: Umm, no because it doesn't affect it just because you're a boy or a girl.

Jess: No, it doesn't affect it because say in, like, sports, some girls like to play football, and some boys like to play netball. So, there's not really anything that one gender is better at.

Eleri: We have three really good mathematicians in our class, two boys and one girl, and the girl does so much maths at home, and I think that the boys do too. And, because the girl likes to play outside too, she likes sports and maths. Some of the boys think that they are rubbish at art. They can do everything, just maybe not as good as someone else.

What would you like to be when you're older?

Jess: I want to be an actor, in films and pantomime.

Eleri: They're turning the old fire station in our town into a cat rescue place. I want to work there.

Tyreese: There's like multiple things I wanna be. Either a footballer, a businessman or a Formula One racer.

Ollie: I have three things I might be. A chemist, maybe an actor or an artist, or a palaeontologist.

Are they all jobs that all genders can do?

Tyreese: They can, but if they didn't like it then they wouldn't have to!

Jess: Normally when you're little you think that you have to be a boy to be a doctor, and a girl to be a nurse. But there's actually a lot of girl doctors and boy nurses so it really doesn't matter.

Eleri: They are just different jobs. To be a doctor, you give people medication and to be a nurse you look after people.

Ollie: Some people suppose that 'a boy can do this', and 'a girl can do that', just because the name might sound more boyish. Like 'doctor' sounds like, you picture a boy, and a nurse you see a girl. Even though they can both do both, it just sounds to us like they can only do one, but they can't.

Why do you think it does sound like that to us?

Eleri: It's like, more rare that girls would play football, but they still can.

Jess: Normally you would find one or two girls in a football team, and one or two boys in a netball team so you would think that. Say that when you're watching football, it's mainly boys.

What do you think it means to be a boy or a girl?

Eleri: It's like, if you say you have a sister – I have a brother – but if you say you have a sister but it's actually a brother, then that wouldn't be true. I think it's just so we know things like that.

Ollie: I think, um, some are shorter than boys but most of them should be taller than boys.

Jess: Probably like, they are either like sporty or they take loads of selfies. Or they're somewhere in the middle. I'm in the middle.

Eleri: Boys like being boyish, playing football.

Jess: Boys think that they are like, more mature, they think they're really cool. Some girls do too, but mostly boys.

Ollie: Some boys might be more daring and adventurous than girls. Like boys might try to climb a tree whereas a girl might prefer to learn to plant.

Jess: Sometimes you could have, like a sister, who is really daring, and then a brother who is really shy and might not like doing stuff like that. It doesn't matter what gender you are, you might be really strong or really shy, or anything in the middle.

If someone was to say something mean about your gender, what would you say to them?

Jess: I would say like, I like football, and if you don't like that then I don't really care. If I like football, I like football.

Ollie: I would say that I can be whatever I want to be. There's no limit to what I can do and what genders can do. There's stuff that is made for everyone.

Eleri: I would probably say that I can choose what I want to do. I wouldn't listen to someone telling me what I have to do.

Tyreese: They have basically covered it all!

Analysis

I had an amazingly mature conversation with Year 5 who repeatedly stated that it doesn't matter whether you're a boy or a girl, but that they could see differences around them in what people supposed that boys and girls should do. They were firmly of the view that it doesn't matter whether you're a boy or a girl; however, they understood that society expects them to behave in different ways. Their aspirations were relatively unaffected by bias, and they couldn't think of any jobs that would alienate either gender. Given that it was a group of two boys and two girls, it was interesting to see how much they nodded along with each other to show that they agreed with what was being said. I think that we underestimate how much our students pick up from their surroundings.

Year 6 – Harry and Ruby

What do you think the biggest difference between genders is?

Harry: Um, well, all there is is parts of your body. That's the only difference, there's nothing else. Your brain is the same.

Ruby: Yeah, like, they just have different parts but you can act like a girl if you're a boy and you can act like a boy if you're a girl.

Okay, what about in terms of your mind? Are boys better at some things and girls better at others?

Ruby: Well, boys can be better at like football but boys can be better at netball but if you put your mind to it then you can be just as good as anyone else really.

Harry: Because if you think about a footballer, not being sexist or anything, but you think of a boy don't you? But say if you think of a ballerina, or say a hairdresser, you would think of a girl which isn't right because boys and girls can be whatever they want to.

Leading on perfectly to the next question! What would you like to be when you're older?

Ruby: I wanna be an actress, like on the telly and be in family films.

Harry: I want to be a paediatrician.

Why?

Ruby: Because I have a passion for acting and I like making people laugh. Like, I make people laugh quite a bit and I like making people happy if they're upset.

Harry: At first I wanted to be a forensic pathologist but then I thought, 'Oh, I don't really get to speak to the patients.' (*giggles*) So, adults when they're injured don't really talk a lot, they just want to stay calm but I guess a way for a child getting out any sadness is through chatting.

So, if anyone said that you couldn't do your dream job because of your gender, what would you say?

Ruby: I would tell them that it's not true because just because a boy might be better than somebody, you can still try your hardest and try to accomplish your dream.

Harry: Well that would be their opinion, I wouldn't really care. I would just go for what I wanted.

Have you ever wanted to do something and not been able to because you're a boy or a girl?

Ruby: Not really no. All my family say just be what you wanna be and no one can stop you or force you to do anything.

What are your top three jobs for men?

Ruby: Well anything really…footballer, hairdresser or an actor.

Harry: Chef…um…cake decorator…and a dancer.

What about women?

Ruby: Footballer. Actress or a teacher.

Harry: A GP. A referee in football. And a shopkeeper.

Do you think that the gender of a teacher matters?

Harry: I would prefer a female teacher; they're a lot friendlier.

Ruby: I don't really mind either. I've mainly had female teachers but I had one male teacher and I could trust him, and I can trust my female teachers so it's no difference really.

Analysis

Talking to Year 6 was a great experience. I currently teach Year 6 and ensure that I have a constant dialogue with them because it can be a time that is integral to their development. The Year 6 pupils that I spoke to were very open about their perceptions of boys and girls and how they should behave, and also extremely keen to make me aware that they didn't think that it was fair that jobs might be thought of as more suitable for one particular gender. They made a conscious effort to try and portray the idea that anyone can be whatever they want to be. Given that they are going up to high school, this is a really good outlook for them to have. Ruby in particular made the point that some boys may be better at acting than she is, but that that should not and would not have any bearing on how good she herself was as an actor; it would just spur her on to do better for herself.

Year 7 – William

What do you think the biggest differences are between boys and girls?

William: Their bodies. The way that they act. Boys are boisterous and girls are quite delicate and sensitive.

How do you think that you learnt to associate those things with being a boy or a girl?

William: I just think that boys do sports and mess around with people. Girls are calmer, basically. That's in school and out of school. Everywhere.

Do we stick to those roles in general?

William: For a lot of people, we do. Sometimes people change.

In school, do you think that boys and girls are better at different subjects?

William: No, unless research shows that they are. I don't think they are. They're equal in all abilities. My classes are top set and they are pretty even with boys and girls.

Do you think that there are jobs that only men can do?

William: I don't know. Like, a lot of women or boys have done something that women are supposed to. Like a first ever female bin-woman, stuff like that. I think it has all been done before.

How do you think that gender roles have changed over time?

William: They've merged a lot because of different influences. Celebrities, social media has taught people to be whatever they want. In the 1900s, a girl would want to work but society said no so she couldn't. But now, everyone can do whatever they want. Celebrities show us that we can do different things.

Analysis

In the first few years of high school, puberty has taken hold and the students that we once saw as cute and innocent are now becoming temperamental and argumentative! The changes that occur in this time are massive and can provide real issues with how the students look at themselves and the world around them. No longer are they oblivious to the troubles that are around in our world, but rather are more in tune than many because they are noticing it for the first time.

William is set in his belief that boys and girls are equal in ability and in what they can become when they are older. He made a great point when he said that all of the roles once for men have now been done by women, leading to the conclusion that there should be equality in the workplace because any gender can do any job. William has had his perceptions influenced by people that he sees in the media and sees this as a positive thing – that celebrities show that you can be anyone you want to be.

Year 9 – Erin

What do you think are the main differences between boys and girls?

Erin: Boys are more naturally stronger than girls are. I think boys tend to hide emotions more than girls do because they don't want to come across as more emotional. It's quite stereotypical for girls though.

What do you want to be when you're older?

Erin: A physiotherapist. I think it's mixed because anyone can do it. It's not stereotypical work. I'd want to do it in the sports sector, so if I had football clients, I feel that I would have more male clients.

If you were a boy, would you want to do a different job?

Erin: No, because there is no reason that a boy couldn't do it, or a girl couldn't do it.

Are there any jobs that you think boys and girls couldn't do?

Erin: No, I think everyone is the same. The only difference is the hormones, so I suppose a man is naturally stronger. I think women have more common sense, so I think they're quite good with problem-solving stuff. Say if you're a builder, having to carry heavy loads, it's better to be a man.

Do you think that genders are treated differently in school?

Erin: Yeah. Teachers are quite...especially in PE, they push the boys more than the girls. Especially if it's a male teacher with sports like football or rugby. It's quite disheartening, I suppose, because you would do just as well as everyone else. If they're not applauding you like everyone else, then it's disheartening.

What do you think the biggest barriers for genders are?

Erin: Sexism for girls. Saying they can't do something because they're a woman, or that they are not capable of doing it. For boys, I suppose they are expected to do more than women, because that's the stereotype. I would deal with gender barriers by saying that it's discrimination and that's not okay.

Analysis

Erin has a slightly different perception from William. She has noticed that boys of her age hide their feelings because they don't want to appear 'too emotional' – an attribute more applicable to someone identifying as female. She has noticed that in one of her favourite subjects, PE, she feels that the boys are pushed more than the girls, something that she sees as fundamentally unfair. As someone who wants to go into the field of sport as an adult, it's then understandably conflicting for her to see that another gender is being shown some favouritism because they identify as a boy.

It struck me that William saw far less injustice than Erin, and I would imagine this will have something to do with how these pupils are treated by the adults around them.

By the final year of high school, many students will have a good idea of who they are and who they want to be. They have a certain level of maturity and are usually ready to go to the next level of their life.

Year 11 – Max

What do you think the word gender means?

Max: I think it's the biological sex of a person. I think there's a clear difference between sexuality and gender though. I wouldn't refer to pansexuality as a gender, that's a sexuality. There's male and female.

What do you think the biggest difference between boys and girls is?

Max: Uh, physical. I don't think that it's any secret that men are biologically stronger. I think it's the way you look mainly. Everyone is different, aren't they? I'm probably different to another lad. I'm probably as different to another lad as I am to a girl.

So, in terms of school, how much of people's ability is based on their gender?

Max: There's much more girls in my top sets than there is boys. I think girls have less going on outside school. A lot of lads are obsessed with football. I think girls are less interested in sports and that has something to do with it.

Are there subjects in school that boys are better at?

Max: PE. Because don't get me wrong, there are girls that are stronger than boys; but generally, boys are quicker, stronger and can throw further. But then again, girls are better at netball so there is a flip side.

What about in terms of academic subjects?

Max: I think that, like, engineering, boys are generally better. I can't put my finger on why. Maybe it's because all current engineers are boys. Maybe girls don't wanna do it. But in terms of academic school subjects, girls tend to be better at them all.

Do you feel like you've been pushed by adults into wanting a certain job?

Max: No, I haven't decided yet. I want to go to university to study economics or computer science but not sure after that. So no, I haven't been pushed into a specific area.

What would be your ideal world in gender equality?

Max: Obviously the ideal world would be that everyone is equal. But not in all ways because if everyone's equal then it turns into communism which isn't good, it never works. Obviously, you can't change biology. Physically, boys are boys and girls are girls. Um, to be quite honest, I just think that obviously women should get the same pay and vote. But there can't always be complete equality because there wouldn't be leaders. Where there are inequalities, I don't think that should necessarily be between genders, it should be between people. Regardless of how they feel.

Analysis

Here, we have yet another facet of the argument of gender equality. Max was confident in his belief that boys and girls are naturally different. He explained that boys are naturally stronger, and girls have less going on outside school. Max made the point that girls are less interested in sports. When looking at Max's answer to the last question, I had enormous respect for how it was relayed. For a 15-year-old to establish that there shouldn't be differences between genders, but rather between people, is a huge philosophical statement to make at such a young age. He understands clearly that there are differences between social classes and education levels and believes that this is where the inequality should lie, rather than between men and women. It's quite a profound statement to make – and sparks the question of, 'Should there be inequality at all?', because if our Year 11 pupils are thinking that people are not equal, then that's quite a large hurdle to get over.

Myth-busting

Again, we look back at the myths that surround gender differences. For this section, instead of focusing on the academic differences between children, we will look at how aspirations are seen in the adult world and how these will undoubtedly have an effect on the aspirations of future generations.

There are still huge gaps in the way that men and women are treated in the workplace. It's becoming more common to see men being favoured over women for higher-powered jobs, which is then reflected in the distance between many colleagues' pay checks. The way that this looks for our children is that it's just one of those things. But that should not be the message that we are delivering to the students in our care. It's not enough to say that no matter how hard you work, or how hard you want it, chances are you're going to be limited by the fact that you are associated with the rest of your gender. This section will show you how these myths evolve and how they are perceived by our students. It will also endeavour to help you negate these myths with hints and tips of how to alleviate aspirational gender gaps in your classroom.

Myth #1: 'Girls are too emotional to handle high-powered jobs.'

As we look further up in a place of work, men seem to dominate the higher realms – there is a 9% gap in the average annual earnings of men and women. So, why does it seem that men are consistently gaining higher-powered roles ahead of women who are just as capable? Some people believe that this is because of the supposed emotional dependence that women possess – something that males are apparently just not ailed with.

It is thought by a surprising number of men and women alike that women in higher-power roles would just not be able to detach their emotions enough to make decisions that may alter or progress their business. This is an incredibly archaic and downright offensive point of view coming from people who should know better. The time should have been and gone where women were thought to be the weaker sex.

When teaching our students that they can be what they want to be, an issue arises as they begin to discover that gender roles are still apparent in the working world – for girls especially. It's the idea that no matter what they do, their gender will still play a role in their chosen place of work.

If I didn't know better, I wouldn't be surprised if we were creating a generation of women with a defeatist attitude when it comes to going for the big guns. But knowing how resilient and strong some of my students are, I have no doubt that they will fight with every morsel of strength to achieve what they are entitled to.

When children see the differences between men and women, which no doubt they will have seen in the media, they will continue to affirm those stereotypes because that's what is being shown to them. It shouldn't take high-profile women quitting their high-paid jobs because their male co-worker earns more than them. It should be a given that your gender is in no way indicative of your performance in a job.

My ideal solution for fixing such a gender-biased view is to educate the children on the current state of the working world, while encouraging them to think about how this will affect them as they grow up.

Lesson idea: The Apprentice

1) Set up two businesses in your classroom. One consisting of boys, the other of girls.

2) Give them a brief, something like 'You need to create, market and sell a product that will fill a gap in the market.'

3) This is the crucial part – don't give them anything else at all. Children thrive off being given free rein and independence to complete a task.

4) Give them deadlines to complete their tasks by and then watch them sell their self-made, self-marketed products.

5) Take them to 'the boardroom', set your class up like a meeting room and discuss the highs and lows of the process.

6) Explore the differences between how the boy-headed team and the girl-headed team coped with the pressure.

You should notice very little difference between the two teams, ergo showing that if someone is given the opportunity, then they will rise to it no matter what their gender is.

Myth #2: 'Boys aren't as good at pastoral jobs.'

It tends to be a common thought among a lot of people that men should not or do not take part in jobs that require them to show a compassionate side. It's common to see throughout history that men were the ones who brought home the money after a long day at the office. Women were stay-at-home members of the family that took care of the children and the home. It stayed this way for a really long time, as Section 1 proved. Nowadays, however, women go out to work just as much as men – a sign of times changed or a sign of a greater need for more money in the household?

Either way, both men and women work to bring home a wage that supports the needs of their family. So why is there still a stigma attached, particularly to men, about working in a certain role?

It's much more likely that we see women in roles such as nursing or primary teaching because of their supposed caring and compassionate nature. This is a form of sexism in the way that it is stereotyping that all men and women need to conform to gender roles that have been around for centuries.

A brilliant example of the other side of this argument comes from a book that I read with my class every year: *The Giver*. *The Giver* is a coming-of-age novel written by Lois Lowry about a future world where patterns of speech are clearly monitored to ensure that no one speaks out of turn. The reason that this book is relevant to this myth is that each person is given their job role at the age of 12. The protagonist's father has the role of 'nurturer': he is a midwife who takes care of children until they are handed over to their assigned family.

The book explains that the elders had noticed that the father had always exhibited signs that meant that he would make a brilliant 'nurturer', so there was no doubt of what he would become.

In our culture, we seem to feel as though men working in pastoral jobs run against the status quo. It's thought by many that men just aren't suited, and this is part of the reason that we have fewer men in these roles. Of course, not all men will want to work in pastoral settings, but I do feel that the choice for them to do so is often taken away.

When I look at the boys in our classrooms, and see them being caring and affectionate to others, it makes me wonder where that stops later in life.

I would strongly recommend *The Giver* to any educator or parent because it teaches our students some brilliant lessons about equality.

Myth #3: 'Some jobs are only for women, and some are only for men.'

Teachers should be women. Pilots should be men. Mechanics should be men. Nurses should be women.

Unfortunately, everyone has a predisposition over what they think that men and women should do as an occupation. When you think of a pilot, most people automatically think of a man. There are female pilots, of course, but when asked about which people would feel safer with, unfortunately, many people say that they would feel safer with a male pilot. The possible reasons for this, I imagine, would be that men are more known as the gender that are less affected by their emotions, meaning that in a state of danger, they would be less likely to panic. That, of course, is ludicrous. I have no doubt that if your plane was nosediving towards the ground, there would be panic no matter what society thinks of your gender.

Similarly with male teachers – especially male teachers of younger children. Some people feel uncomfortable with the thought of their child being under the care of a male professional. Why? Because their instincts don't provide them with enough emotional range? The point that I am trying to make here is that if a person has chosen a certain path, has gone through all the necessary training and is enveloped with passion about what they do, then who has the right to tell them that their gender makes them unsuitable for the job?

As for our students, they too will have predisposed ideas about what jobs are suitable for what gender. These views don't generate themselves; they are shared and passed down by the adults and people in positions of trust that surround them. It is then our duty to show our students that despite what society may dictate about what you can and cannot do, if you are passionate and driven then you should still fight for what you want.

Lesson idea: The Rescue

It will be one that you have heard before but this activity can be really valuable at any age for children to explore how useful people are in society, regardless of their gender.

1) Explain that there are a group of people trapped down a mine: a male teacher, a male nurse, a female pilot, a female mechanic, a male beautician and a female lorry driver.

2) State that they have limited supplies to keep them going. Give each character a background – children, family, responsibilities.

3) Ask the children who they would save, in an order, and get them to give reasons as to why they've made the decisions that they have.

Through this activity, you will begin to notice different belief patterns of your students. Feel free to step in and challenge views and allow for

healthy debate. **This activity will allow children to expand their own thinking within the space of collaboration and the safety of a made-up scenario.**

Myth #4: 'Men and women have different brains.'

Now, in one sense, this isn't actually a myth. But the connotations and stereotypes that come from this statement are as farcical as they come.

Yes, men and women do have slightly different brains. But so do some women and some men. It's not fair to say that any two brains are the same, just as it's not fair to say that women's and men's brains are fundamentally different.

Some studies have shown that men's brains perform better with logical tasks, and women's with more literacy- and language-based tasks. This is a fair representation of the split that we see in our school data as discussed in Section 2. What this doesn't show us is that men and women are biologically predisposed to take on a certain role in life. So, it doesn't make sense for us to assume that one's brain capacity has anything to do with their gender.

Another interesting debate here lies in the time-old argument of nature versus nurture. Are our brains really that different? Or are we responding to the external factors that affect our way of thinking? Do men and women act differently because their brains are wired to do so or is it because we are societally programmed to behave a certain way?

Imagine a classroom where there is one boy in a class full of girls. How would we expect that child to perform in relation to their peers? In terms of aspiration, we would assume that the boy would grow up wanting to become something, but what that is will probably have been affected by the external influences that has gone on through his education, rather than through the wiring of his brain. The same goes for a female student in a class full of males. Would this child be more inclined to take on a role that is usually aimed at men?

For our students, wanting to fit in with what is classed as normal is usually a sure thing. Few children want to stand out for being different, unless they have orchestrated it to be that way. It's here that we need to be careful to not create a 'normal'. As far as the next generation are concerned, there shouldn't be a normal that everyone needs to conform to. I have no doubt that they will be a damn sight better than the standards that we are still forcing on them.

Let your students make their own mind up about how they want to use the brain that isn't like anyone else's. Create an environment where there is no normal, no status quo. They'll thank you when they grow up and feel uninhibited by the 'wiring of their brain'.

Myth #5: 'Women aren't as competitive as men.'

This is often used as the reason that men gain higher-paid jobs in the workplace. Now, imagine if this is true, that women are just naturally not as competitive. Where would this leave us?

Competition in any sense is exciting, I'm yet to meet anyone who doesn't like to engage in a bit of healthy competition, occupation or otherwise. No one likes to feel like they are inferior, let alone that they would allow for people to step over them to get to the top.

Is it that we are conditioned to believe that women are less competitive? I think it might be. Maybe to ensure that women don't try to aim for the jobs that are seen as beneath them because of their gender. I think that people are still stuck in their views as to what the roles of gender in society should be, and that judgement will be passed on by those who try to upset the apple cart. It may almost seem like a threat if women were to get in on the competition for work that is viewed as being entirely for men. Known as the weaker sex in almost every culture, surely losing out on a job opportunity to a woman would be embarrassing for most men – consciously or not.

In terms of the message that we are delivering to our students, I've already mentioned how both boys and girls respond well in lessons to competition.

There are some handy tips on how you can promote competition in your class so that this myth isn't around for the next generation.

Myth #6: 'High-performing women are always full of themselves.'

I have had the great misfortune of being the subject of this myth personally. After delivering a training session to a room full of school leaders on something that I consider myself to know a lot about, I felt invigorated. I loved that people were listening to what I was saying, especially given my age. I consider myself to be fairly high-achieving in life, because I have a drive for it.

I was in school a couple of days later and a colleague from another school informed me that her headteacher had said, 'That Hollie needs taking down a peg or two, doesn't she?' My response was to stare, bemused, into the eyes of the teacher who was sharing this information with me. Taking down a peg or two? Not the most complimentary of reactions to something I had worked hard on and built myself up to deliver.

It got me thinking, is it common for women to receive such stunned reactions if they are seen to be doing well?

What a sad world we live in where we can't appreciate someone's strengths because of their gender or position. It's really no surprise that our girls are growing up quieter and less confident than the boys in their abilities when all around them, grown adults are behaving like they're still on the playground.

It's not a fact that high-performing women are full of themselves. But just as anyone else who is succeeding in their job, they have every right to have their head held high. I am a confident person, but in no way do I give off the air of thinking that I'm above people and it made me really sad to think that this is what was thought about me.

Something to remember:

As educators, we need to draw the line for our students at what is an acceptable way to behave in society. This doesn't mean teaching them that they have limits and that they shouldn't strive for more for fear of judgement – this goes for any gender.

Classroom strategies for bridging the aspirational gender gap

We have discussed different ways that children see their own and others' aspirations in school, and we've looked at some not-too-true 'facts' that are always hanging around above our heads. Now it's time for us to look at what we can do in our own classrooms to ensure that our students are getting the deepest knowledge and understanding that they can for them to be ready to go out into the big, bad world of work.

1. Explore different job roles

'Why don't you become an air hostess?'

It's common in our classrooms to label specific characters with the roles that they will take when they grow up. When we affirm their belief that their life is leading in one particular way, it's hard then for them to detract from the path that you have subconsciously put them on.

Educating our students about the different kinds of job that they can have when they are older is not something that isn't done. It is done. It's done by way of careers days, where students can come in dressed up for what they want to be when they're older and professionals will be invited in to give advice.

For this strategy, make it a regular occurrence that the discussion of possible future aspirations happens. Keep reminding your class that they can and will achieve, so long as they keep working hard for it; unfortunately, things don't tend to just fall into your lap while you're sitting there idly.

Give your students examples of job roles that don't conform to the norm. Introduce them to the idea that a woman can be a pilot, or mechanic, or engineer; and that men can become hairdressers, dancers, cooks. Broaden their horizons because some children will have been deprived of what some of us take for granted. It sounds obvious, but it's often forgotten about.

Some lesson ideas for promoting non-stereotypical job roles

1) **Debate.** Get your students all involved with a debate about whether you would feel more confident having a male mechanic or a female mechanic. Talk about the different sides, assign a proposition and an opposition and watch people surprise you. If you really want to look at the gender element, get the boys to fight for female mechanics and the girls fight for male mechanics.

2) **Interview.** Use the roles that your class can come up with to hold mock interviews. Pick a range of jobs that could be assumed to be for one gender more than another. Ask probing questions, preparing them for real life and then get the rest of your class to respond to the interview. Peer assessment – tick!

3) **Play.** This is more relevant for teachers of younger children. Use the wide array of dressing up clothes that you undoubtedly have in that big cupboard of yours to show the children how occupations take people of all shapes, sizes and genders. Allow them to act out scenes as different characters.

4) **Teach.** Make use of the fantastic technology in your school by having the students create vlogs on how you could achieve a certain job. Get them to conduct questionnaires and research into how one achieves whatever is needed to fulfil a specific job.

5) **Map.** Nice basic starter: get your students to map out what they think are jobs that are better suited to men or women. Ask them to explain their choices and allow others to respond. You should end the

lesson with everyone understanding how other people view gender roles in the workplace, and then you can move on in your planning with ways to promote or change the views of your students.

2. Bring in the professionals

'There's no connections for our students to make with the outside world.'

When we look at our students, we see them emerging into older, more mature people who will soon be functioning members of society. Our job is to teach them about the ways of the world, skills that they will take through their whole life.

We have just talked about how we can encourage our students to think of jobs that are uninhibited by gender. Jobs that they can want to do without fear of their gender stopping them from doing so. We still live in a culture where there are desired people for certain jobs. Employers tend to have someone in mind when writing a job description. This is not to say that they know this person; simply that they have a preconceived idea of what they are looking for. More often than not, this person will have a gender – it's difficult to picture a person without one.

In school, our students will have a limited experience of the working world. I remember one of my students asking me what I wanted to do for a job, and she was aghast when I informed her that teaching her was my job. 'Oh, I didn't think of it like that!' – and I don't think many of our students do. When they think of jobs, they think of the jobs that are around when they are children. Doctors, scientists, firemen, police officers. All those jobs that are echoed around childhood through books and television programmes.

For this strategy, we will explore how you can use connections that you have in the local community to invite visitors in to encourage the children to think outside the parameters that they have had since childhood.

Making connections

1) **Call around.** Make a few phone calls to businesses that you know are near you that provide some kind of service. Most businesses will be happy to send over one of their employees to talk to your class. After all, it's great advertisement for them!

2) **Ask parents.** Many of our students' parents have exciting and ambitious jobs. Some don't. Ask a variety of parents to come in to school to talk to the class about their experiences in the workplace. The students – younger ones especially – love having parents in the class.

3) **Ask children.** Ask your class who they want to see. They'll tell you what they're interested in and you can see whether it's in your reach to make that happen. These are the guests that are going to make the biggest impression on your pupils because they are the ones that have asked to see them.

NB: All of my guests were asked the question, 'How much do you earn?', as I cringed in the corner of the classroom. You don't ask, you don't get!

3. Talk about it

'We live in a place where there isn't much around.'

All places are different, but this shouldn't mean that we give our students a different experience of the world than other schools. The area in which your school is situated may well be less developed than inner-city schools, but that doesn't mean that there aren't opportunities around that can be taken.

If you work in a community where there is a particularly high percentage of parents who don't work, then it is kind of put on you as the teacher to ensure that the child realises that there is more out there for them. Children will not grow up with high aspirations for themselves if that's not being echoed at home or in school. Better to have it pushed in one of those trusted places than none.

Imagine being a child in your own class who feels like there are only certain jobs that they will be allowed to do. A great book that shows the significance of us being able to choose our own careers is *The Giver*, by Lois Lowry (I've mentioned it before, I know!). The book shows a community where people are simply assigned a job when they turn 12 years old. They are observed through their lives and then at the cusp of adulthood, they are given their assignment, which stays with them throughout life.

The book asks your students to think about how fair this is. Every class that I have read this book with are astounded by the fact that the characters have no say in their future career. In my experience, this has led to my classes understanding that the fact that we make a choice about what to do with our lives is a privilege that should not be taken lightly.

Conversation starters

1) **'How might you feel living in a world where your career is given to you?'** This question provokes thoughts and engages the children in debate. They start to assess their own choices in life, compared to people who have none.

2) **'If you had to make a choice right now, what would you do for the rest of your life?'** This allows students to think, on the spur of the moment, what they would like to do. It's then useful to keep this conversation going by asking what would be needed to achieve that – getting them acquainted early with training and qualifications that will be needed.

3) **'How do different jobs give you different qualities of life?'** This is always a great discussion, with pupils hopefully understanding that unless you're an incredible footballer, you probably won't make a lot of money as a football player. This isn't about dulling down a child's dream, but rather asking them to think about the things that they value in life: money or happiness.

4) **'Who do you think curbs your ideas on aspiration?'** Allowing students to speak freely about who they believe would have an effect on their future career enables them to wonder about whether these effects are good or bad. If parents are pushing a child in one direction, is that always a good thing?

5) **'Who can help you get to where you want to be?'** Asking children this question gives you an angle to suggest that you yourself may be able to offer some assistance. By telling students who is available to them, we often broaden their minds to comprehend that there is more help out there than it may first appear.

4. Journey back

'What were the ideal jobs when I was growing up?'

As we saw in the first section of this book, women and men in the past had very different ideas about what jobs boys and girls could do as they grew up. A woman's purpose was to make and take care of the family whereas the man's purpose was to provide for that family by going out to work.

In our modern day, both men and women commonly go out to work, possibly due to the need for more income, possibly due to people realising that women were just as equipped as men to perform jobs. As we saw in the interviews with the children, they have set ideas as to the equality between men and women in the workplace. Very few believed that jobs were only for specific genders, and most believed that jobs were not defined by gender. Yet we are still faced with a few minds that hold the belief that careers can be affected by your gender.

This strategy is to explore how job roles have changed throughout history, showing our students that where once there was gender inequality, there are now more opportunities provided for all genders. It involves looking back at how women's education was limited to housework skills, and then forward to the rich curriculum that we provide them with now. It also shows our students that men are no longer required to provide for whole families, leading to the understanding that neither a man nor a woman is necessary in order to be a full family – something that needs to be explored with children, given the number of single-parent families.

Some of our students will not have learnt about gender in history, and this can often be the first step to ensuring that gender equality becomes a reality for their working lives. Students will be quick to recognise how unfair the roles of the genders were in history and teachers should take advantage of this to draw parallels with issues that we are still faced with today: pay gaps, opportunities and sexual harassment in the workplace.

Ideas to kickstart a revolution

1) **Look at the suffragettes.** A great subject to look at for gender equality is the suffragettes. The suffragettes provide a brilliant focal point for explaining how people campaigned for change, and how those campaigns were sometimes fatal. Allow your students to research and perform PechaKucha presentations about their findings.

2) **Explore the world wars.** During these conflicts, women took the helm in factories at home because the men weren't there to provide the food and money that was so desperately needed. Invoke the minds of your students by getting them to rank the importance of the jobs that the women performed.

3) **Ask about child labour.** In Victorian times, children were chosen to complete work such as mining and chimney-sweeping. Weigh up the pros and cons of having children perform tasks rather than women – there's more than you think!

4) **Become Georgian.** For a day, become a Georgian society. The girls sit bored in their houses, disempowered, waiting for their husband to come home, and the boys can complete all the work that is needed. Nothing gets the students going more than a bit of unfair treatment – they'll undoubtedly have something to say!

5. Teach what is acceptable

'But I don't think I can broach these subjects with the children.'

In a world where we hear about a new sexual harassment case in the news every week, it's imperative that we educate our students about what is and isn't acceptable in the workplace. Given that it's famous people who are being publicised as being sexist, who's to say how many cases go unnoticed in all other walks of life?

It's super important to note that it isn't always women who are the victims for this sexual harassment in the workplace: men are also victims – often in workplaces that are dominated by women.

Let's just think about what constitutes unacceptable behaviour. Is it that someone makes a comment over what you're wearing? Or is it when a person is grabbed against their will? The fact of the matter is that sexual harassment can take many forms, and it often depends on each individual victim's view on what is and what isn't acceptable.

Given that our students are forever seeing sexual harassment and abuse cases arising in the media, this isn't a subject that they are unaware of. But they do need to be made aware of the different forms that sexual harassment can take. We don't want our pupils going out into the big, wide world thinking that certain things are okay to do or have done to them.

It's a good idea to think of sexual harassment as anything that makes you feel uncomfortable in the workplace that is of a sexual- or gender-based nature. It might seem like it's not our place to raise an issue like this in the classroom, and it can often be uncomfortable; but in the grand scheme of things, it's much more sensible to broach it early so that it can be easily spotted if they were to encounter it. Just as we teach our students to listen to instruction, to use good manners and to try their best at everything that they do, we should also therefore teach them acceptable ways to behave in the wider world.

Lesson idea for teaching the acceptable

1) **Starter:** Give your students some sticky notes to write down what they think is an example of sexual harassment. Ask them to stick them onto the whiteboard and then read out a few for discussion.

2) **Main activity 1:** Use the sticky notes and ask the students to rank them from most extreme to least extreme and see if there are any differing opinions. If there are, use these as debating points to challenge and rationalise.

3) **Main activity 2:** Get some role play out of the old teaching bag and get the students to write short scripts showing the run up to a possible sexual harassment. This allows them to see how these things can start and develop into more. Ask the students to stop the action when they think there is an integral turning point. Allow them to step into the action and improvise how the scene could go otherwise.

4) **Plenary:** The students should be able to show their role plays to the rest of the class and explain how they have decided to change the situation. The session could end with a recap of what sexual harassment can look like and how it can be challenged – and ultimately, avoided.

Conclusions

This section's aim was to bring to light the views of the children and the aspirational differences that our students have. Through conversations with students, I gained a deeper understanding of how they view themselves at different ages and what this means for them as they grow up. Students change throughout their education, which is only natural, but as teachers we can see that those changes can sometimes have detrimental effects on how they view themselves and how they view the world.

Aspirational differences are the variations in how our students want to develop later on in life: what they want to do, who they want to become and what they want to achieve. This section wanted to explore what, if any, differences our students face in terms of aspiration because of their gender. When conducting the interviews with the students, I did not envisage what

I wanted this section to look like. I just wanted to talk to current students about how they felt being a certain gender affected their lives. At each age, the views of the students varied quite a lot. At the younger years, the children didn't seem very affected at all by gender and this was quite refreshing. At Year 3, however, we started to see different ideals coming out with the belief that boys and girls can only do certain jobs that are dictated by society. Year 3 were quite set in their beliefs about how boys and girls should behave – a characteristic which changed again by Year 4. The Year 4 pupils interviewed were a mix of boys and girls, with the girls stating that they thought that being a boy would be better because they get to play better games. As stated in the analysis of this conversation, we now see that at age 8, some children believe that society's expectations of how genders should behave is dictated by some higher power, or the government. This is a great example of how our pupils are led to believe that they need to act in accordance with their gender from as young as 8. Obviously, with gendered toys and television shows too, we know that they are subjected to these rules from a much earlier age. In Year 5, I had an incredibly mature conversation with a mix of boys and girls. They showed wisdom beyond their age when talking about how society leans towards genders to complete jobs, something that I wouldn't have expected them to pick up on. However, they were quick to banish any idea that certain genders could be unsuitable for certain careers. In Year 6, the pupils again were very equal when talking about different genders. They understood that there is equality, but both agreed that they wouldn't let this affect their future aspirations, which was great to hear.

In Year 7, the pupils are still quite naïve but are already noticing the changes around them. The pupil in Year 7 identified specific characteristics of boys and girls, stating that boys are boisterous and girls are sensitive. It's interesting to think where these characteristics have come from – whether they have come from first-hand experience or from expectations from teachers or the media. In Year 9, the girl interviewed expressed concerns over the equal treatment of girls in PE. She had seen first-hand that boys were given more attention from the male teachers, perhaps on the unfair assumption that boys are more interested in sports. In Year 11, the student explained that he believed that girls were just as intelligent as boys, but that perhaps they wouldn't be suited to careers in the area of engineering – because there are no female engineers. This view comes from a lack of positive role models in schools for women. This isn't to say that the role models shown should be female, but they should allow students to see the breadth and scope of different careers before they make up their mind. The female members of Max's year may also hold the belief that women cannot work as a tech firm CEO and would therefore not entertain the thought, narrowing the pool even further in terms of women in higher-powered jobs.

After the interviews, we looked at busting some more myths. Again, these myths came from things that I had heard first-hand growing up and in my professional life. Ideas such as women being unable to handle higher-paid jobs, or men not being as good at pastoral work, help to build up a picture in the minds of our students that they are limited in their career path by the gender that they have chosen. By allowing these myths to spread and develop, we are limiting the aspirations of our pupils, something that was demonstrated by the interviews. Some of the children didn't believe that they could do a certain job because of their gender, and all children expressed an understanding of other people believing that genders limited your ability. The myth-busting section should have given you some applicable and useful ideas of how we could combat the myths from within our classrooms.

In the final section, Classroom Strategies, we looked at ways to broaden our students' horizons, helping them understand that they can be what they want to be, as long as they work hard for it.

My aim in this section was to make teachers aware that we sometimes need to talk to our students about this kind of thing, rather than ignoring it and letting them figure it out for themselves when they're older. They are never too young to start thinking about what they want to be; in fact, they love to talk about it. By talking to them and getting their own ideas on how genders can be seen in society, you can find any discrepancies early and teach to abolish them. Education is the first tier of understanding; how are you expected to pick up an unbiased view of the world if you haven't been given an unbiased view of it?

I was very lucky in my youth to have supportive parents around me. Not all of my teachers were so supportive. Some had very open views over what

I could and couldn't do, while others were limiting their minds to not see beyond gender barriers that had been put up in front of them. As teachers, we are hugely influential for our students, and they take what we say as truth. It's an incredibly great power to hold, so it's crucial that we use it for the right reasons, and not for the gender 'ideals' set out by society. By teaching them that they can be what they want to be, regardless of their gender, we are teaching them that the power of their future is in their own hands.

Even at the highest level, organisations including the BBC, HSBC and the NHS have been found to have significant gender pay gaps. In education, many are concerned that government data shows male teachers are £900 a year better off than female teachers, and men in leadership are doing the same job as women but are paid up to £4000 more.

As BBC Education Editor Branwen Jeffreys writes on the BBC website, 'Why do schools have a massive pay gap?' (2018).

'By law, all companies in Great Britain have to report their gender pay gap to the government by 4 April [2018]. So far, 2516 of an estimated 9000 companies have reported their figures, including 181 primary and secondary schools. Of those, only 11 pay women more than men.'

In November 2017, the Department for Education's *School Workforce in England* census data reported that there were 947,000 people working in state-funded schools in England, with over 451,900 of those teachers in the classroom working full time.

Year-on-year statistics show that four out of five school employees are female, with 73.9% of (full-time equivalent) teachers working in the classroom being female. The gender workforce is split between primary and secondary teaching, with 33,700 teachers who are men and 207,700 who are women at primary level, and 74,500 men and 132,300 women at secondary level (Department for Education, 2018).

With so many women entering the teaching profession, schools should be more thoughtful with helping female teachers during the most challenging years when starting a family – a period of time where, new DfE research suggests, schools may lose them not only from their school, but from the profession as a whole.

Research by the National Foundation for Educational Research (Worth et al., 2017) found one in six secondary school teachers in England working part-time, while 'a greater proportion of primary teachers are female, who are more likely to work part time' (Worth et al., 2017) and those working part-time are more likely to leave the profession.

From the classroom floor to the upper echelons of our education system, the gender pay gap exists between men and women doing the same job.

Ofsted, the organisation responsible for school standards, reported a 'difference in employees' average earnings from April 2016 to March 2017' (Ofsted, 2018a). The watchdog published its gender pay report in March 2018, finding that 'although there are more women than men in each [pay band] overall there are more women in more junior grades, where pay is lower'. The percentage of female staff within its own organisation is 63%, while the Civil Service is higher than the average of 54%. The question is, even if Ofsted's pay gap compares favourably with the Civil Service, why does it exist in the first place? Worse, why are civil servants who are inspecting schools receiving bonuses? And gender aside, why is there such a lack of diversity at Ofsted senior level? (Ofsted, 2018b)

According to an Ofsted spokeswoman, 'to achieve a bonus for the year's performance an individual must meet their financial objectives, and will have consistently exceeded expectations throughout the year in terms of delivery of projects and leadership and management' (Roberts, 2018).

In September 2018, after 10 years of producing anonymised appraisal reports for Ofsted inspections, and justifying pay-related decisions, I made a freedom of information request for an anoymised sample of Ofsted appraisal targets at leadership level to learn a) what types of targets were set and b) what gender differences may exist. Despite having shared these duly on demand with all Ofsted inspectors during various school inspections, it seems that Ofsted is not willing to do the same with the general public.

A lesson for us all is that we should all be committed to fair pay, irrespective of gender and organisation, and that those in positions of power and influence should be leading by example.

1. When you were young, did anyone ever suggest certain careers to you based on your gender? Why do you think that is? How could it be changed for the future?

_____

_____

_____

_____

2. In your experience, what focus has been put on the way we gear students towards their future careers? Does gender play a role?

_____

_____

_____

_____

3. How often do you complete classroom activities that question societal expectations of gender?

_____

_____

_____

_____

4. How might you plan for more activities that address the issue of the gender gap? Why not make a list and share it with the hashtag: #GenderGapBook

_____

_____

_____

_____

siblings can have an effect on how different genders behave, or grow up expected to behave. More and more families have more than one child, and this can provide a brilliant role model for the younger child. However, if that child doesn't feel as though they are behaving how they are expected to, or performing to the same standard as their older brothers and sisters, then this can cause them to become reclusive and untrue to who they feel they are, which unfortunately leads to resentment in most cases.

The last thing that we will look at in this section is how influential markets and organisations dictate the behaviour of different genders. All around us – in supermarkets, high street shops, advertising boards, religion – there are indicators that all genders should still be behaving in a certain way, subliminal messaging that confirms to our students that their gender makes them who they are and tells them how they should behave.

I will endeavour to give tips on noticing issues that arise and ways to stop them in the hope that, as teachers, parents and people in positions of trust, we can create an open and accepting world for the children in our care. We are the catalysts for change for our students and children. When you picked up this book, you had already realised that an irreversible reaction is needed to create something new.

Social media

If we break down the term, 'social media' would suggest that it is a way for people to socialise with each other. That seems like a fair representation of one of the fastest-growing phenomena in the modern world. Social media sites have age restrictions on them, the youngest being 13. Why is it then that as a primary school teacher I am having to deal with issues that have arisen from using social media? This section will explore social media, how it affects our students and how it can sometimes reaffirm gender stereotypes.

Background

Social media first attracted a mainstream userbase in the early 2000s, by way of MySpace. People all around the world could communicate by way of pictures and posts about their lives to share with whoever they wanted. It was new and exciting, far more personal than writing an email – but much more invasive than writing a letter. People didn't have to know your address to send you something; it was right there on a plate for you. Being young, I remember being about 8 when YouTube and Facebook first reared their heads. I was strictly not allowed on social media, and I didn't get the internet until I was 13 – a lot later than some of my friends. I was 'given' the internet as a present on my 13th birthday and I was allowed on for an hour a night after 7pm when it was free. I kept to these rules and didn't make a Facebook account until I was 14, and allowed to. I know that a lot of my friends had Facebook before me; but for us, it wasn't that big of a deal – we were all over instant messaging on MSN.

Social media provided a platform for people to meet people all over the world from the comfort of their desk chair. Twitter came about in 2006; a platform for people to communicate in a limited number of characters. But again, all over the world.

More and more social media platforms emerged after that. The whole world went mad for this new way of looking into everyone's lives at the click of a button. It became very easy to see into someone's mind because they'd given you the privilege. That's their prerogative – I see things on social media now that make me cringe and wonder why anyone would share such intimate details about their life; but I suppose, in a way, it's good. It is the ultimate form of freedom of speech.

In terms of our youth, they are now almost expected to be on social media – like it's a requirement. No longer are we waiting for new, quicker ways to communicate with others. More and more come out every single day. Children are brought up around adults who spend hours scrolling through news feeds and timelines, laughing at memes or funny videos. It's no surprise that children are wanting to jump onto the digital bandwagon before sites think it's okay for them to do so.

I love social media. I'm active on Facebook, Twitter, Instagram and I even have a YouTube account. I'm not saying for one second in this chapter that social media is a bad thing and that we shouldn't use it. What I will be saying is that there are dangers associated with it that we all need to be aware of.

Primary schools: the discovery

Often, the first introduction to social media happens at primary school age. Children are exposed to social media from a really young age. Like I said, they are persistently surrounded by adults that spend a whole chunk of their free time on the sites so it's no wonder that children want to get in on that action.

'Ah, they're mature enough'

I know that from teaching in a primary school in North Wales that children of primary age do not adhere to the rules that are in place to stop them from using social media. Age restrictions are in place on all major social media sites, and they are there because the content on these sites is not deemed appropriate for people under that age. More often than not, parents will know that their children have social media accounts, and they try to convince themselves that it is okay because they monitor the settings or have access to the account. My job is not to tell people how to parent their children; I wouldn't know the first thing! However, parents should really take note of these age restrictions because you can't be checking all of the time. There will be a time where a child has seen or heard something on social media that they shouldn't have.

'Have you got Snapchat?'

Something that I find interesting is looking at what sites primary age children are interested in. From what I've gathered, Snapchat, Instagram and YouTube are the main contenders up to 11 years old. Snapchat allows for quick messages or pictures to be sent and, if chosen, automatically deleted after ten seconds or less. As soon as Snapchat surfaced, that rang alarm bells for me. Three seconds is plenty to get an eyeful of something that you didn't want to see. There are settings, of course, and you have to add someone to have them in your Snapchat contact list; children tend to be more accepting than adults of people that they don't know – especially if it's a friend of a friend.

YouTube is another solid favourite. Children spend hours and hours watching videos of vloggers who earn exorbitant amounts of money for not doing an awful lot. They breathe in everything that these vloggers say and want to be like them. This is a great tool if the vlogger is a good role model – but cataclysmic if they're not. For the record, you have to be 18 to have a YouTube account, and without an account, a lot of the inappropriate content is blocked.

Instagram is a popular forum for posting selfies. Today's generation are far more confident to post pictures of themselves online – usually covering their mouth or only showing half of their face. It's quite the spectacle to watch an 11-year-old pose for a picture then edit and filter it beyond recognition. Depending on your privacy settings, you can choose who is following you.

'But, I didn't think anything would happen!'

Like anything, social media comes with its risks. Given that children under 11 are using social media, it needs to be noted that they are at risk. Just like being out after dark, the internet is full of dark people and dark places.

One of the biggest issues that faces primary school children is cyber-bullying: a form of bullying that takes place wholly (or at least for the most part) online. This can stem from abuse on a picture that's been posted, or a nasty message sent through the private messaging systems that are present on most social media sites. It can be the sharing of private information or a group set up to victimise one person. Hopefully it's not too often, but we do experience bullying in our schools. The difference online is that the child can hide it for as long as they want to. It's a private event that happens through the clashing of screens. It's much easier to hide a feeling of hurt than a physical bruise.

or started eating less, sometimes this can signify that someone has said something unkind, usually online, that has made them re-evaluate how they want to be seen.

5) **They're more defensive than usual.** Any teenager will be defensive if you question whether they are doing something wrong. If you know a teenager who is defensive in a way that you haven't noticed before, make sure that they know they can talk to you about anything.

Social media is a great way for all people to communicate when they're not physically around each other. It's just important that for the children we raise or educate, we need to remember the risks that can arise.

Television, film and music

Everywhere we look, we are surrounded by film, television and music. As a culture, we tend to love audiovisual entertainment. The fact that we can sit in front of a screen and watch anything we want is taken for granted very often; and without us realising, it occupies our mind for a lot of the time.

Some of us schedule our days around what is on the television; if you're fortunate, you can record live television to watch at a time of your choosing. Going to the cinema to watch the latest blockbuster brings a more social aspect to our watching – and on a screen that's way bigger than any we could have in our homes. Houses are sometimes judged by the size of their television, the quality of the speakers in the room and the cable provision that it has. We watch comedy, drama, horror, documentaries, soaps. We watch almost everything that is put in front of us simply because it's there for us to do so. We are entertained by people all over the world, right from the comfort of our living room sofa. What we don't realise perhaps as much is that television, film and music dominate our perceptions of the world around us. 24-hour news channels and music being played around the clock on streaming services mean that it's almost impossible for our screen-obsessed youth to avoid.

In the past, televisions were scarce and only the richer households had one. When I was little, we had 5 channels – but there were even fewer before. Picture houses would show limited films each month and music was played on the wireless. We have come such a long way from going to watch television at one of our friends' houses because they had a better aerial.

Gender in entertainment is a big issue. In recent times, scores of women have been announcing to the world, very bravely, that their trade is an incredibly sexist one. Everyday sexism is becoming increasingly visible: gender bias in pay and job opportunities is a common form of discrimination, and countless women continue to speak out about sexual assaults perpetrated by men believing that it was okay. Women are being abused online for standing up, and whether or not you believe that what they are saying is true, you have no right to subject anyone to a barrage of abuse online.

As for the children and students we have in our care, a lot of their ideas of how men and women should behave come from something that they have seen on television. It provides a seemingly unbiased view of the world and children are quick to take on roles that they see on the screen or hear on the radio. This chapter will look at how primary and secondary children can be affected by what they see on television, looking specifically at the roles that men and women play in television shows aimed at them. I will explore how modern music is fraught with gender bias and how this is perceived by children.

Television and film – primary school children, age 3–11

'What's on TV tonight?'

Television aimed at children of primary age tends to be on after school on the mainstream channels, but on all of the time on cable networks. The television shows that are aimed at these children help to form the child's view of the world.

A child, male or female, will always choose to watch what makes sense to them and sparks an interest. As a child, I loved watching *The Demon Headmaster* and *The Worst Witch* when I got home from school. I loved school, and both of these series were based in a school. I also love *Harry Potter*, so a school of witches was massively interesting to me.

At primary age, children are most receptive to what they see and hear around them and this will shape their future perceptions of how men and women should behave. If a child is only seeing women who need to be rescued by a man, then that child will form the preconception that women are weaker and therefore need to be saved by men, who are less prone to shows of emotion.

These stereotypes are further enforced when we look at cartoons where the males will be unnaturally ripped with muscle and the females will have a waistline that a mouse would envy. These unrealistic portrayals of gender make children feel as though there is something wrong with them. Children will want to alter themselves, to make themselves look and feel more like the characters that they see on television.

'What do you want to go and see?'

Films are another way that children have their minds filled with how men and women should behave. Blockbuster films are still full of gender bias. While there are more films that are demonstrating characters who act out of their 'norm', we are still confronted with unequal emotional portrayals of characters.

For example, the Disney films are working hard to abandon some of their meek and fearful character portrayals of females; however, there are still princesses that need to be rescued – they just have a bit of sass to go along with it. *Brave* and *Frozen* are just two examples of a princess story wherein the princesses are self sufficient and independent. Similarly, male characters in these films are almost universally unemotional. A man gets into a fight far more often than a woman in a Disney film but both genders give unrealistic expectations of human strength. We are filling our children's minds with the idea that girls can't fight, boys can't cry. It's really no wonder that the rate of children suffering with low self-esteem is rising.

Male characters often give out misguided messages to their young viewers, encouraging the belief that men should behave in a way that supports their wife and children without showing any signs of weakness.

In schools, we can combat this by pointing out characters that defy these gender stereotypes. Discuss with them how different the characters were in the film they watched over the weekend and then talk about whether these roles could be played by a man or a woman. Talk to them, allow their receptive brains to think about these questions without fearing that they can never live up to the unrealistic and demanding nature of their favourite film character.

Television and film – Secondary school children, age 11–16

'It's past the watershed'

At secondary school age, our students will watch a variety of television shows, both with their parents and without. With the emergence of Netflix and Amazon Prime Video, and not to mention YouTube, there is no end to what they can watch.

With this much television available to the children, it's no surprise that their world view is affected by what they see on TV.

In their teenage years, our students go through the biggest change in their life so far: puberty – a time where nothing feels like it is going their way and they desperately look for something that they want to become. It is at this time that they associate themselves with a certain style and assert their interests.

Television that teenagers watch tends to fall into two categories: children's or adult's TV shows. There seems to be very little aimed at teenagers on mainstream television. There is an issue that arises here. Whereas the children's shows are often too immature for teenagers, the adult shows provide content that is possibly not appropriate for a 14-year-old to be watching. Given that these children are affected by the characters and the themes in these shows, it's crucial that they don't feel the need to be like the people that we see on the screen. I stopped watching soap operas in my teens because I was fed up of something bad happening all the time.

I became paranoid that this could happen in my life – *Emmerdale* made me fear a plane crashing into my small North Wales town. I understood very quickly that this was unlikely, but it did make me realise how much of an effect TV had on my cognitive state.

If the teenager is watching a television show that is too old for them, especially if it has a sexual or violent element, this could encourage the viewer to want to be perceived as sexual or dangerous in order to become more popular with their peers. This is the same for both genders.

Somewhat limited by what they are engaged by on television, teenagers are hooked by videos on YouTube where than can hear the rants and ravings of someone their age who has a platform for their voice. Sometimes, these aren't the best role models. Many vloggers talk about positive body image, such as Zoella. But others give a pessimistic view of the world that isn't necessarily helpful to their viewers' mental health.

'It's only a 12'

Certificates on films are there for a reason, just like the age restrictions on social media. The content in the film will be inappropriate for those under the age. This isn't the case for every child, some are more susceptible than others to anxiety.

Gender roles tend to be more explicitly prevalent in adult films; one franchise that springs to mind is *American Pie*. Of course, not all classifications are perfect. The *James Bond* series – with the sexist spy who loves guns, fast cars and women – gives a pretty biased view of how men and women should behave, but all but one of the films are rated as a 12A or lower. I love the *James Bond* films, don't get me wrong, but they don't really give out the best message for our children!

Horror films tend to be the genre of choice for a teenager trying to fit in. Sneaking into a viewing of an 18 film would definitely get you some popularity points in the social hierarchy. In these films, more often than not, a woman will need rescuing from a man. Alas, the perpetrator is usually a man! Doesn't seem fair, does it? This creates a culture of thinking that anyone who can do something bad to you is probably male and if you're female, you stand no chance.

Films like 2017's *Wonder Woman* provided a refreshing view of a woman as a superhero – but still, she was dressed provocatively and was dolled up to the nines. It gives off the impression that even if you are busy saving the world, you still need to look your best.

While television and film have come a long way towards making gender more equal on screens, there is still an astounding amount of gender bias facing our children every single day. Do your bit as a teacher or parent – point out the appropriateness of what they're watching. Try to provide them with a wide breadth of gender figures for them to aspire to.

Music

Well, where to start with music and gender. The stereotyping in some music is clear. Beyond clear. Women and men are both portrayed in music in a way that is demeaning to them. Especially prevalent in rap, grime, hip hop and R&B, women are portrayed as meat, often parading around in next to nothing in music videos. Men are seen as being thugs with weapons and drugs. I am a fan of all music, and as adults, we can appreciate that the purpose of overly sexual music videos is for entertainment; but it upsets me to see that our children are watching these videos, looking for an anchor for what is classed as normal and acceptable. The music industry is overly sexualised, and this leads us to have to watch our children at school discos grinding and pelvic-thrusting. It shouldn't happen.

Children will learn and repeat inappropriate song lyrics because that's what we do with music. I remember putting '7 Years' by Lukas Graham on in class, and hearing all of my class sing the line 'By eleven, smoking herb and drinking burning liquor' was enough for me to run back to my desk and turn the song off. Songs that we wouldn't expect to be giving bad examples are all around us and we have to be so careful. If a song doesn't have an explicit rating, in theory it should be okay for children to listen to – but quite often, this isn't the case.

Growing up, I listened to all kinds of music. I love it. With the exception of dance music, I will willingly listen to anything. But only when we flick on a music channel do we see what our children hear every single day. They are being taught that it's okay to behave like the artists and speak how they speak.

I would never deprive the children in my care of listening to music because it's a brilliant medium. However, taking note of what they're listening to and how this might affect their world view is a must if we want to promote an idea of gender equality in their minds.

Peer pressure

What is peer pressure?

Peer pressure is the encouragement of one person to another to behave or dress a certain way to appease others. This encouragement can be positive or negative, but the term usually comes with negative connotations. In schools, we teach about peer pressure with the example of someone offering you a beer or a cigarette. We teach that our students should say no to any peer pressure – something not particularly easy to do when one's social status is on the line.

Our students are consistently at risk of peer pressure. I remember being in school and being called 'frigid' because I didn't want to conform to the overtly sexual standard that was deemed the 'in' thing at the time. It made me feel rubbish. I knew that I didn't want to be 'one of those girls', but I also knew that my popularity (not much, but still) was at risk. Peer pressure can take many, many forms.

It's a form of bullying, yet it's done by people that you supposedly trust. Friends are most commonly the root of peer pressure. And it's a lot harder to say no to your friend than to some random person. No one wants to lose face around their friends – especially not children.

In school, everyone wants to fit in. This is more easily noticed the higher we move in education. Foundation Stage children seem little phased by what their peers think; but at the upper end of primary education, peer opinion can be damning, with everyone wanting to fit into a clique by the time that they reach secondary school. In secondary school, our students meet an array of people that they have never met before. This is a hugely exciting time where students tend to change and mould into the people that they will become in later life. I know from my own experience that for the first two years of secondary school, I flitted between groups trying to find my niche – which I did in Year 9, and they stayed with me until after we left. For those first two years, I changed more than I could ever say. I tried to fit in with groups that I wouldn't have entertained before. I did things that I wouldn't have done before or after. But that is all part of growing up. Peer pressure was just a fact of life.

What does peer pressure look like?

Peer pressure can take many forms and be about many different things so we will look at it at different stages of education.

Primary school

In primary school, peer pressure may not be as noticeable. Most peer pressure goes on without the teachers present – they're too smart to let you catch on. Even in primary school, there are pressures that shouldn't be there, leaving children to feel as though they have nowhere to turn.

At this age, children have a sense of what is right and what is wrong. They also have a good sense as to what is different between them. Some children come from lower-income families, they don't have the same nice clothes, and they're not able to go to the cinema at the weekend with their friends. This can sometimes be a source of peer pressure. The desperateness to fit in overshadows the understanding that the child feels about their own home situation. Rather than thinking about the issues going on at home, the child can feel that it's their parents fault that they don't fit in, leading to resentment.

Another peer pressure hotspot is ostracising peers that don't conform to the majority's idea of 'cool'. Even up to age 11, children know what they think is cool, and if someone doesn't adapt to that, then it's very easy to make them feel lonely. Note here that the peer pressure isn't on the ostracised child, but rather on the peers that are doing the abandoning. There will always be one or two ringleaders on the school yard that dictate how others are perceived. This might be the child with the loudest voice, or the one with the best home life. It might be the class clown or the one with difficulties in the family. It can be any child that you have in your class, and you probably have one in mind. This child will, for whatever reason, want to alienate other children, creating their own little beehive to rule.

Secondary school

Peer pressure seems to be more prevalent in the secondary sector, where the students are at an age where they are desperate to fit in by any means necessary. At the ages of 11–16, our students will experience some kind of peer pressure. Some peer pressure comes from what they have and what they want. Many children come from better backgrounds than others and our society is still entrenched in class. Peer pressure to have nicer clothes or better gadgets can cause issues in the home and could even go as far as to encourage illegal activity if the child is really eager to fit in.

Other types of peer pressure seem to have more sustenance in terms of changing a whole persona. Everyone can remember a time that they were offered a drink of alcohol, or a cigarette. In that moment, we all made a choice. You either took it or said no, and faced the consequences. That still happens today, where some students will offer something up that they know they shouldn't have. It tends to be done in groups, where the ringleader will make an offer which, when refused, will lead to taunting or humiliation. Peers will join in so as to not put themselves in the same position. While some might say it's character building, for some of our students, their social perception is at the root of their self-esteem. Many students with lower self-esteem will do things to make themselves appear like someone they're not because it's cool.

This becomes dangerous when the peer pressure is leading to something that could harm or criminalise a person e.g. taking drugs or having underage sex. Sometimes the need to fit in outweighs the risks of partaking, so as educators, we need to do our utmost to educate our students about the dangers of peer pressure.

Who does it and why?

There are two types of people involved in peer pressure.

1) The 'pressurer'

2) The 'pressuree'

The pressurer in this scenario will be the one who is most respected in the group. The one who makes the rules and punishes those who don't follow them. It may be that you know such a child from your classes. The question that I would like to ask would be, 'Why are they doing it?' Surely, making someone do something they don't want to can't give too much gratification? Or can it? My theory is that the pressurer makes themselves seem above everyone else because they have deep-seated issues in themselves. I once had a child who, I had no doubt, was peer-pressuring others. I made it very clear that I was aware and ended up building a really good relationship with the girl, who actually had very low self-esteem. No one is controlling because they're happy in their life. They grasp for control of their peers because chances are they don't have control anywhere else in their life. Being the leader gives a great sense of hierarchy, a status that needs to be kept up in case someone comes to knock you off your perch.

Think of a child that you know that has these characteristics. Ask yourself about their home life, the size of their family, their school history. I can guarantee that you will find something that puts a label on their behaviour. The pressurer will persist in their reign until someone explains to them that it isn't the way to deal with their problems.

The pressuree is the student who will give in to peer pressure. They may struggle and then give in, or just give in straight away to avoid the hassle.

There are more pressurees than there are pressurers. These are the students who have particularly low self-esteem – meaning that they have a low opinion of themselves – and therefore feel they have nothing to lose by giving into the pressure. This child may feel as though they are different, or less than their peers – something that can quite often be orchestrated by the pressurer. Our students feel as though they need to slot into the pressurer's ideal in order for it to stop. In my experience, students who have less stringent rules and routines at home are more susceptible to peer pressure because there is no one there to teach them that certain things are the wrong choice.

Again, think of a child that you think may be vulnerable to peer pressure. There has to be at least one. Have you noticed any child being 'a loner'? Someone who doesn't have the closest home network? I know children who are desperate to fit in with the status quo and it breaks my heart that they don't think they're good enough as they are. Be the person who tells them that they are.

The difference in peer pressure of genders

As we have already established, boys and girls are different. But this doesn't mean that our treatment of them should be dictated by this. Boys and girls tend to be affected by different topics of peer pressure as they move through education. We will look at what issues boys tend to be affected by, and the same for girls.

Boys, as a general rule, don't show emotion as much as girls. This is a social expectation that is ingrained in the minds of the male members of our society from a young age. This does not mean that they are not as vulnerable to peer pressure. If anything, it's more dangerous because they will hide how they feel.

Boys tend to be more at risk of peer pressure or social ostracisation if they display any feminine attributes, such as being interested in dancing or hanging around with girls. With the need to appear as masculine as possible in an education setting, boys with more feminine aspects will undoubtedly be faced with judgement and ridicule by some. This leads to the male wanting to conform to something that is more pleasing so that the dent in their social vehicle is repaired. This can lead to really low self-image, because the individual doesn't feel that they are free to be themselves – they feel they have to create a more pleasing version.

According to some studies, boys are more likely to succumb to peer pressure with more risky behaviours such as underage sex or drinking. This may be because these feats are seen as a show of rebellion and masculinity. It's common for teenage boys, especially, to brag about their sexual conquests to other boys to dominate their group.

Girls tend to be more likely to be influenced by peer pressure when the topic is their own appearance. If a girl feels as though she is larger than the rest of her group, then this can cause her to change her eating patterns to fit in. This peer pressure may come from others directly or from comments made that would highlight the difference, such as, 'Are you having chips again?' This is obviously a dangerous road to travel down with the prevalence of eating disorders that our students experience, both male and female.

Girls may also be prone to peer pressure about their sexuality. If a girl refuses to take part in sexual activity, they are mocked for being prudish; and on the flip side, girls who will engage in sexual activity may be branded with derogatory words for their supposed impurity. The effects of both leave scars that will stay with them for a long time.

LGBTQ pupils should be included in all of the above. Many LGBTQ students feel as though they are particularly at risk of peer pressure due to their sexuality or gender identity. This is something that should be taught at schools at all levels. Children should not be made to feel that they should expect ridicule because of something that they have no control over.

Tips for promoting healthy minds

There is no point in saying that peer pressure should stop. Because it won't. It's been around for as long as humans have. So, let's focus on something that we can change. As educators or parents, we have the ability to ensure that our children understand that peer pressure is not a rite of passage.

1) **Reiterate that there are different types of people.** No one is the same as anyone else. This doesn't mean that we should treat them in any different way than we would treat our friends. We have students of all races, sexualities, religions, ethnicities, ages, intelligences, backgrounds. That's such a lucky environment for us to be able to work in because preaching tolerance should be easy. Explore the variations of people that we meet and make it clear that you would never treat them differently.

2) **Explain what peer pressure can look like.** Many of the students that we teach may think that peer pressure is only when you're offered an illegal substance – I know that is what is still taught in PSE. We may have a mix of pressurers and pressurees that don't even know that what they are doing is peer pressure. My advice would be that you don't make it clear that you are talking about the students in your class, but more like a generalised discussion about something that you heard or read about over the weekend. That way, it's less accusatory.

3) **Explore why people might feel the need to pressure others.** Like we have discussed, people may feel the need to pressure others to gain some control over their own life, where elsewhere they feel like they have none. This might spark an idea in your students that they themselves fit this profile, or that they know someone else who does. Make it clear that this person is not always the bad guy, they're just making bad choices that they can choose to stop at any time. There's no such thing as a bully, just a person who bullies.

4) **Suggest ways to deal with it.** Saying 'no' doesn't seem like an option. Especially not to children. They are still trying to find themselves, and by saying 'no', they feel as though they are putting themselves in the firing line for humiliation. Saying 'no' isn't necessarily the best way to deal with it. Teach the children that they can try and turn it around: 'Thank you, but don't you hate the smell of smoking?'; 'Na, I'd rather wait 'til I'm 18 – it'll lose it's fun otherwise.' If you teach a child to stand up to their opponent, and that it is okay to do that, then chances are they won't be alone. Others will see that they are strong enough to disobey and may well follow suit.

Peer pressure can be crippling for the children in our care, so let's do what we can to minimise the risk by finding the root and providing coping mechanisms.

Familial conventions

In our modern society, families come in all shapes and sizes, with all the variation that you can imagine. We see mixed-race parents, same-sex parents, single-parent families, opposite-sex parents and just about every combination of the above! It's no surprise that children have very different upbringings from one another, and with that comes different gender patterns in children. In this section, we will explore how the structure of different family types can have an effect on the gender identity of a child.

Families with same-race, opposite-sex parents

What I mean by this is families that consist of a mother and father and which do not fit into any of the mentioned families above. This is not to say that this is the 'norm' but it is the picture that we most associate with families. What we may find with children who come from this sort of home life is that the child may feel like they need to follow in the footsteps of their parents because that is the right way to do things. If the individual is female, then they may feel as though one of their purposes in life is to grow up, find a husband and have children – that's fine, if the child wants to take this path in life. But if the child doesn't, would this be a problem for the parents?

If the child is male, they might feel the pressure to be the one who goes out and fulfils the work in order to get money to support his wife and children. These pressures are often not directly pushed on the child but can have an effect on what the child deems as normal.

Given that our students spend time with us while they are still developing into functioning members of society, it's no surprise that their views on gender come from their parents, with whom they spend most of their time, and us as their teachers. It is therefore no surprise that children from opposite-sex families will probably have developed their ideas on gender roles based on the fact that they have a mother and a father who have specific jobs within the family.

In addition, families that conform to the above structure will often agree on political and social matters within the home, leading to the child hearing and subsequently agreeing also.

Single-parent families

There are so many reasons that a family may become single-parent so there's little point delving into the cause. Speaking from a personal perspective, being raised in a single-parent family for most of the time, I lived with my mother and my younger sister. I visited my father and my other family twice a week, but for the rest of the time it was the three girls. That is how we referred to ourselves and how others referred to us.

For me, living with a single parent wasn't anything odd. It wasn't until I reached secondary school that I realised that I was a minority in my friendship group. It didn't stop me from coming to school looking presentable or bringing in enough to eat for lunch.

For some children, their gender identity can be shaped by having a single-parent family at home. We would rely on my grandad to come and help us fix things that were broken in the house. So even though I had a view that I was no different, we did seem to lack that 'male' element of the house that made me feel as though a man was needed to complete the house. Of course, this isn't true. Families mould to fit what is needed to make a successful household.

Children's views on their gender are cemented by their parents; if a child is raised in a single-parent setting then it is common for that child to behave like their parent in terms of their gender. If a male child is raised by his mother then it's not unreasonable to think that the child would display some more feminine attributes, and the same for female children raised by a male. We conform to the people around us, even as adults.

Families with multiple children

Most families in the UK have more than one child. We tend to see students move through school, ending up teaching their brothers and sisters after them. Sometimes that's a great thing; sometimes not so much! Parents that provide their children with brothers and sisters are less likely to be the only factor that shapes their child's view of the world.

Older siblings can have a real effect on the way that a child views themselves and their gender identity. Siblings will almost always pass their interests onto the younger siblings who are excited to be just like their big brother or sister. If the older sibling is reluctant to share interests or views on subjects, then the younger can feel as though they aren't as good. Many younger siblings feel pressure of having to live up to the expectations set by the first child. It's often a lot to live up to so the pressure is not unreasonable. As teachers and parents, we need to make it clear that all children have the right to make their own mind up over who they want to be. If the individual is supported by parents and siblings at home then they are more likely to turn out with a healthier mind than those that are neglected.

It's not right to say that individuals with older siblings of one gender always behave like a certain gender; however, if a female child has older brothers then it's more likely that that child will exhibit more masculine features, and vice versa for male children with female older siblings. It seems that children learn the behaviours that they use through life by watching the male and female role models in their life –looking this way at a sibling, who is closer to their own age, can give a younger child a better idea of how they should behave at this age according to their gender.

Low-income families

It is suggested that children who come from a low-income background are far more aware of their family's financial issues than children who come from homes with better income. It seems that in low-income households, parents are quicker to talk about difficulties in front of their children – perhaps as a way to excuse why the child may not have as much as others, or to staunch some anxieties by sharing the burden. It is understandable that low-income families would want to do something about it, but quite often they can't.

Studies have shown that most low-income families that have two parents are quite rigid in their views as to what genders should be. The societal constraints within the family in terms of gender are made clear to the child and they are expected, quite often, to conform to these stereotypes without question. Similarly, if a low-income household has specific political views, these are also most probably shared by the child and repeated in the classroom.

This is not to say that the families are not giving their children a fair chance to experience the differences that we have in our world, but rather that the children don't have the same opportunities as others to get out and see the world.

With the emergence of Free School Meals and the Pupil Deprivation Grant that accompanies it, many children from low-income households are having their horizons broadened by complimentary trips that allow them to see something that they wouldn't have been able to previously.

In terms of gender, parents that hold more of a traditional view of the family may push the idea that men and women should have separate and different roles within the family. It's interesting to see this projected in a family where neither parent works but the child still has views on what a woman and a man should be able to do. The child will have heard this said somewhere at home for it to have been instilled in them. As teachers we need to be aware of children who believe that gender stereotypes are the be-all and end-all of their future life.

Families with same-sex parents

Families with same-sex parents are less common than other families. Where two women or two men choose to raise a child together is something that is relatively new to our society.

Many same-sex couples will fear having a child together because of the risks that could befall that child going through the education system.

Individuals who disagree with this family ideal often make their views clear to the children and this could cause resentment from the children towards the parents.

Children only come up with ideas on how a family structure should look from the adults around them, e.g. teachers and parents. This means that in order to make sure that each child is given the same opportunities, we need to educate our students on the importance of acceptance and tolerance, at the least.

Many same-sex couples will have been asked the question, 'Who is the man?' Now, how damning is that to a child who doesn't realise that their family is anything other than normal. Just because a family has two parents of the same gender, doesn't mean that the family should conform to being 'male' and 'female' as parents. If anything, children of same-sex families stand a better chance at dispelling gender stereotypes.

In schools, educators need to reassure all children that just because they may have certain constructs at home by way of family, this doesn't mean that any one is the right one. Often, talk of LGBTQ families will evoke a negative response from some of our pupils – it is often more vocal in primary school than in secondary. I have had children in my own class exclaim, 'Gross!' when I've mentioned a same-sex family in a PSE lesson. When asked, 'Why gross?', the child literally couldn't answer the question, leading me to believe that it wasn't a first-hand response but rather a learned response from someone they know.

Gender roles in work

Children's views on gender roles are characterised by their parents or home life. I will now explore how the occupations of these parents could also have an effect on the aspirations of the children. As I said way back in the introduction, my parents both had super-stereotypical jobs. Dad works for a luxury car brand and my mum is a beauty therapist. My step-mum was a legal executive. So I had three role models from which I could take my views on what I wanted to do in the future. As it happens, my experience of aspiration varied as I grew up. Starting with my aspirations to be Indiana Jones, I then wanted to be a barrister, then an actress and then finally a teacher. Doesn't seem like I was at all influenced by my parents, except for the desire to work in law like my step-mum.

For some children, the occupation of their parents will have an effect on what they would like to do. It's not uncommon for those in low-income families to follow in their parents' footsteps and work in labour or trade. It's also not uncommon for children of business-oriented families to follow their parents into big corporations.

In my view, aspirations are based around the push that comes from the parent. If there is not a lot of push, then the child is less likely to want to go out and achieve more than their parents did. However, if the child comes from a supportive and goal-oriented family, then they are more likely to have higher expectations of themselves.

There will never be a time when everybody wants to enter higher education, because that's not how our society works. However, by giving our children examples of female and male role models for gender we create more chances for them to see what they could become, and why they should want more for themselves.

Families come in all shapes and sizes, and they create the children that we have the good fortune to teach. Each child will have their own preconceptions about gender roles that stem from the home, and we should take note that we have the ability to ensure that all children see gender as something that does not dictate how they need to behave.

Societal expectations

In this section, we will look at how a range of things outside of any category are also serving to gender our children from a very young age. All around us are signs that boys and girls should be raised to behave a certain way and it is through these constraints that we still have gender divides in the 21st century. Again, we can't stop these things from

happening, but we can go a long way to ensure that our children are not sucked into the gender stereotyping black hole that we were.

Gendered toys

All children play with toys in their childhood. Some toys help to bridge the gap between things in reality and things that are okay to play with – real hammers and kitchen sets are obviously not safe, but toy ones are fine. The issue arises with toys when they are directly aimed at either boys or girls. Advertisers and businesses thrive off making toys that are aimed at separate genders because it makes them money. Parents who are conscious of gender roles are often drawn to these gendered toys because they don't want their child to be seen as anything other than normal. For advertisers, this makes a pretty penny when they can also come out with a toy that is for the other gender.

Given what we can take from their advertising, boys' toys tend to consist of cars, train sets, footballs and building equipment – all the things necessary to become the manliest man one can be. Boys are brought up being surrounded by toys that reaffirm the fact that they are male and therefore can only play with things that would assure that. By limiting female experience with such toys, we are also limiting their belief that they can do anything boys can do. It quickly affirms that girls shouldn't take an interest in labour jobs such as mechanics or building work. Toys are just smaller, safer examples of things that we encounter in day-to-day life.

Girls' toys tend to be pink and consist of dolls, nail kits, arts and crafts and cooking sets – again reaffirming the belief that girls are born to have children and look after the house. Now, if a child wants to play with those toys then by no means should that be stopped. I had all of the above toys as a child and loved them all. However, when we are aiming them at female children exclusively, we are limiting a child's ability to see beyond the gender confines that we have put into place for them.

In schools, it is then our duty to make sure that when we have toys (particularly relevant for the Foundation Stages), we use toys that can be explored by any gender in order to create a sense of equality in aspiration.

Building blocks that can be constructed into anything the imagination wants, dolls that are a mix of different races and sexes. Dress-up clothes that can be worn by anyone. These are all great ways to show the children in your care that it doesn't matter if you're a boy or a girl, you can play with whatever takes your fancy!

Clothing

Children's clothing is a real bugbear for me. Walking around any shop with children's clothing just opens your eyes to what a gendered society we live in. Clothes entrenched in the tell-tale colours of blue or pink. People buying baby clothes before they are born so that they aren't mistaken for a gender that they have not decided upon yet. When toddlers, children are dressed in colours that announce their sex to the world without them even knowing what that means. It doesn't seem fair. Yes, they're children. But it doesn't mean that their identity should be decided before the time that they can speak.

One of the most concerning matters surrounding clothes for children is the slogans that appear on them – things like 'I'm too pretty to do maths' or 'Boys will be boys.' It's not too much of a jump to see why our children are growing up thinking that the differences between their genders is noticeable. The slogans featured on these clothes are reinforcing gender stereotypes wherever we go and they are widening the gap between boys and girls. (Whatever happened to everyone in dungarees outside climbing trees? What a great time that was!) Making our children walk around with such an item of clothing on is about the same as stamping 'I'm a girl/boy' on their forehead in permanent ink.

The issue that arises is that parents do not want their child to be seen as different, which is understandable to an extent. But how far will you go to make your child unhappy wearing something just to appease anyone who might have a different opinion?

Some retailers have decided to ditch the boy/girl labelling already, which is a great move forward. However, even this has received criticism from people saying that children are too young to have made an informed decision on their gender anyway. My response to this is: are children too young to be wearing mimics of the clothes that adults wear in the name of fashion? Too frequently, I see young girls walking around in little heels, with makeup on and a short dress. Gendering clothes is just as bad as over-sexualising them – both are huge issues that are often brushed under the carpet.

Let your child decide what they want to wear – it's not the adult who has to go out in something they have been dressed in.

Advertisements

No one enjoys an advert. My parents go so far as to pause a television show for 15 minutes so that they can skip through all of the adverts that interrupt their viewing of the latest drama. However, advertisers thrive off putting loads and loads of adverts on the children's channels. Whose child doesn't sit there writing up a birthday shopping list in the break for *iCarly*?

Advertisers are great at what they do. They sell products. They sell them especially well to children who feel the desperate need to have what they've just seen on TV straight away as if it's the missing piece from their life.

Adverts for children can be incredibly sexist. One example that always stands out for me is the advert for Nerf guns. Typically blue, the guns are shown in adverts with young boys running around and firing at one another. What makes me laugh and cry simultaneously is the fact that this advert is almost always followed by the female equivalent of the Nerf gun: a nice, pink crossbow aptly named 'Rebelle' – we wouldn't want to think that this is the same as the masculine boy toy! The fact that these adverts follow one another just goes to show the tendency of toy companies to perpetuate gender divides from bringing out gender-specific toys. Generally speaking, if a male child asked for a Nerf gun, parents would be on board with that. But would it be the same for the female market? No, that's why they brought out a female specific. Very few parents will want their child to be parading around with a toy that isn't suitable for their own gender.

Adverts are very clever in getting you to believe what they want you to about a product. Just look at the steam mop – most households wanted one when they came out! The problem with adverts for children is that we are constantly reassuring children in our classrooms that gender doesn't matter, that you can be what you want to be. Then we are almost always stabbed in the back with weapons just like the Rebelle crossbow.

There is a way that we could combat this for the students we teach.

How to beat the advertisers at their own game

1) **Debate.** Have your class stage a debate on whether they think the advertising ploys work. Get them to write detailed speeches for and against gendered advertising and hear both sides of the argument. Nice little oracy task too!

2) **Study.** Get hold of a catalogue and rip some pages out to look at more clearly. What techniques are used to sell to girls? Boys? Have them analyse why this might be and even look at costs of similar toys for different genders.

3) **Test.** If you can, get some children to bring in toys that they have at home and explore how they are different. Draw out measurements, measure them, assess their usefulness.

Sports teams

I firmly believe that all children should have a chance to experience sports outside of school. Lots do, which is great. But the majority of these are boys. Sports like football and rugby are dominated by men, which sends out a certain message to the children that we teach.

I have girls in my class who would love to compete in football or rugby teams and when asked why they don't, they answer that 'There's just a boys' team; they don't really like me playing with them.' Now, this isn't the sports team's fault; it's a lack of tolerance. What I would like to see is more being done to combat sexism in sport.

In recent times, women's football teams have been receiving more publicity, which is brilliant. The hashtag #thisgirlcan trends all the time, with women sharing their stories of how they got into sports and encouraging others to do the same. It's a brilliant movement that we should get behind for all children to become healthier, confident individuals.

There seem to be stereotypes associated with people doing sports. For men, it's a sign of health and fitness. Yet still for women, competing in sports that men compete in labels you as something quite different – rough and rugged, and not particularly feminine. Many girls will continue to feel reluctant to take part in sport until it is made equal for all. Who made the rule that men can't play netball, or girls can't box? Oh, no one did. Then why is it that we still find ourselves under these constraints that are dictated by people who have no authority or right to dictate them in the first place?

Do your students a favour: encourage them to get out and try something new rather than sit there with their face in a screen. Get them to try something out of the norm. Take them on trips to unorthodox places: climbing walls, gorge-walking, kayaking. Give them a love for sports that will outweigh any kind of hesitation that they might feel about being judged.

More needs to be done to combat the sexist attitudes that are still prevalent in sports. Teachers need to step out of the shadows and tell their children that sport is good for you, no matter what people say about it. This is especially relevant in secondary schools where girls no longer feel like they want to take part in sports, preferring to complete fitness activities in the gym where they can do their exercise in a less-public manner.

Sports are a great way to meet people; don't allow children to be thwarted by outdated ideas that only some genders can do some sports.

Equal opportunities in work

Children that we teach will grow up aware that men and women still don't receive the same treatment in the workplace. If nothing is done about this, we will be raising a generation who believes that they are limited/entitled to certain jobs because of their gender.

In workplaces today, men are more likely to receive promotions over their female counterparts. Now, it's said that this doesn't have anything to do with gender but it seems to happen a little too often for it to be anything else. In 2016, the Chartered Management Institute and XpertHR released research stating that men are 40% more likely to be promoted to managerial roles than women.

Pay gaps are also noticeable, especially in bigger corporations. As children grow up, they will be aware of these gaps. We don't know whether this will lead to a decreased level of motivation for girls who think that they will never achieve as much as their male counterparts, 'So what's the point in trying?' Or will it lead to a revolution in terms of women standing up and saying enough is enough? Currently, we hear more and more about how companies are almost being forced to reveal the gender gaps in their businesses. Named and shamed, to say the least. It shouldn't have to come to this, especially not when we are supposed to be setting an example to the next generation of thinkers.

As time moves on, I have no doubt that men and women will become more equal in the workplace. But until then, as educators, we need to make sure that our children know that whatever the gaps may be, they should never give up trying. Before we know it, we will have a generation who is determined to make things fair once and for all.

Conclusions

This section has outlined some of the things that our children are facing when not under our jurisdiction. It's not enough to only dispel gender stereotypes in our classroom; it needs to extend further than that as much as it can. By gaining an understanding of the things that go on around our students, hopefully we can help them to create a future that is free and fair.

As we have seen, it's not always entirely down to us to save our students from the gender issues that are still at play here. We teach our students that it's not okay to treat someone badly just because they're different. We teach them that tolerance is not a choice and that acceptance should be at the forefront of their minds when they meet people.

When they then step out of our care and into the sometimes-unwelcoming arms of the big, wide world, who is there to teach them that it's okay to be different, it's okay to not feel the same as everyone else and that it's certainly not a problem to be a specific gender?

We have looked at how social media can have a real negative effect on children from a young age, especially when it's unsupervised. These are platforms that we as adults have grown accustomed to over time, and now seem like the norm, a rite of passage for all – including children who aren't old enough to deal with some of the content. Social media can be fantastic for keeping in touch with people, and it can seem overly critical of the world to say that children shouldn't be allowed to use the sites. But unfortunately, there are people in this world who take advantage of parent's naïvety in believing that their child just wouldn't be that gullible.

We explored the role that television, film and music can play in the development of the gender identity of our students and children. All around them, they are faced with stereotypes of men and women that they feel they have to conform to, music lyrics that blatantly denote some unpleasant ideas about different genders. With children who are desperate to fit into what we class as ordinary, we are allowing them to continue in a way that can be detrimental to their development. It's not rare for me to have conversations wherein a ten-year-old will try to tell me about a horror film that they watched with their big sister, or a song that they listened to which isn't appropriate. And every single time, it makes me cringe. I'm not saying that I never watched or listened to something that wasn't appropriate to me, but I am saying that I wished I hadn't, because I then wanted to be just like the people that I watched in films – women who were possibly not the best of role models (such as Julia Roberts in *Pretty Woman*).

We looked at what exactly peer pressure was, and how we might promote this in our classrooms or in our homes. Peer pressure is one of those things that will always happen, but it's not always just going to be one of those things that we bow down to and accept as okay. Peer pressure can have serious implications for the children in your class. You might notice changes in a student who is ordinarily very quiet: marks and grades slipping, absences – and before you know it, they morph into someone that you have never met before. Noticing the signs, and noticing them early, is paramount to ensuring that, at least while they are in your care, peer pressure doesn't take hold in your presence.

This section also examined how different family structures can have an effect on a child's view of themselves and their wider world. Living in a society where we have such an eclectic mix of families is great, and it provides us as teachers with a whole variety of students from different backgrounds. The differences in these families come to light sometimes negatively when parents unintentionally – or sometimes intentionally – pass on their own ideals to their children, who in turn bring them into the classroom. It's not our place to tell parents how to raise their children, but it surely falls under our jurisdiction to ensure that in the classroom, the fair ideologies stay, and our students are provided with a full and unbiased view of society.

We then approached the subject of what society demands of our young people. There is a wide array of topics under this heading and all of them are just as important as each other. But just knowing that these topics can influence a student's view of themselves can go some way to dealing with issues that may arise with self-image. To take something as simple as toys for children: baby dolls are great toys, but surely a reminder that a woman is there to look after children; and toy guns can be fun, but do they promote the idea that boys are violent? Advertisements deliberately, it seems, instil stereotypes into the still-developing minds of children and they carry these to adulthood. Clothing is created to be for different genders, and I can't help but think about the child in my class a few years ago who didn't feel right in their own skin because of these types of pressures.

I wrote this section – even though it's outside of my work, not to do with education – because I thought that it would have been remiss to omit some of the biggest causes of gender inequality in our world. I don't want my students growing up believing that they have to conform. I've used that word a lot because it perfectly covers what young people have to do until they find where they want to be in life. I want people to take note of what has been said, and as an educator, to do what you can to make sure that you are widening the horizons of your students to see past the images that are projected into their subconscious minds every day of their life.

No one should feel as though they need to behave in a way that someone else dictates to them. They may not be conscious of it, but we can use our powers of teaching to show that it's never okay. Whether it's as obvious as peer pressure or as subtle as a pink t-shirt, make them aware that these things go on for them. That people are stuck in the past, sometimes without even realising it. Make them laugh at the ridiculous attempts to try and keep the genders separated in children. Ask them to think for themselves. They'll thank you for it.

1. How often are issues such as social media or peer pressure addressed in your school other than through assemblies?

_____

_____

_____

_____

2. Do you feel like you do enough to challenge the stigma surrounding mental health for all genders in schools? How could you do more?

_____

_____

_____

_____

3. Make a list of what we can realistically do as teachers to address the gender gap from inside our classrooms. Share it with the hashtag: #GenderGapBook

_____

_____

_____

_____

Conclusions

Hairdresser or Footballer? Bridging the Gender Gap is a book about gender inequality. It's a toolkit of how to become a bridge-builder. It's an excavation of some of the most fundamental building blocks of our society. But most of all, it's a catalyst for change.

Why this book?

I wrote this book for a few reasons. The first being that it is topical at the moment. Now, this doesn't mean that I wanted to publish a book on gender because it will sell loads because everyone is talking about it. It means that I wanted the best possible opportunity for people to consider gender equality through the eyes of the next generation and through the words of someone who works with them day after day. All over the media we see people stepping forward and announcing their difficulties with being accepted because of their gender. Unequal salaries, job opportunities and sexual harassment are just part of the female side of the issue. For men, we see more and more mental health issues and men not feeling as though they can express their emotions without being seen as a societal aberration.

The next reason was because of injustices that I have experienced first-hand. I was bullied in secondary school for not being considered to behave as I should, not acting 'like a girl'. I was subjected to ridicule for being a 'tomboy' and caring about my education. I was called a lesbian, which led to some unpleasant individuals proclaiming that everyone should turn away from me in the changing rooms for PE in case I took a peek. My secondary head of year told me that it wasn't fair that they had done that – but made sure I understood that they were right in what they were saying, that homosexuality is wrong and that I should try and behave differently.

The third and probably most important reason that I wrote this book was because I stand in front of my class every day and wonder how they see themselves, how they feel they fit into what is classed as normal. Everyone wants to be seen as normal, especially as a child about to go to secondary school. I wrote this book because I wanted to make sure that I have done my part to ensure that my pupils never have to feel like I did. I want teachers to think about how they are portraying the world. I want them to be honest and fair and give their students a fighting chance in a world that is full of injustice.

The relationship between the second and third reason for my writing this book has been the driving force behind it. No one should be made to feel anything other than what they, and they alone, class as right for them. I want to stand in front of my pupils each day knowing that I am filling them with the positives that the world has to offer them and teaching them not to accept anything less than that.

My experience

When I was a child, I desperately wanted to be an archaeologist. I went through my schooling and gradually lost my drive for it. It wasn't interest that I lost, but the belief in myself that I could do it. I went through a lot of difficulties in high school and then in university that meant that I felt that my gender identity was an issue with the people around me. I felt like an outcast, I felt as though I didn't fit in with what everyone else thought was normal. I didn't want to be different. I changed myself to try and suit them and very quickly I became someone that I didn't like, and that the people who knew me the best didn't like. I realised then that it was time for me to be myself, because the people who cared about me liked that person, and their opinion was the other one that mattered to me.

I started my teacher training and realised that I was not the minority. As a woman, I was in the majority. This is when I first noticed the injustice that can often be around in education. That there are far fewer male primary teachers, more men in government for education. I began to question why that was. I knew plenty of men who were good with children and enjoyed teaching. And after asking some questions, I received my answer. Men are less inclined to teach at younger ages because it's not part of their blueprint of life. They are expected to complete more manly jobs, even now.

As a qualified teacher now, I still face adversity. We all do. There are more male headteachers than female, and yet more female teachers than male ones. How do these two statistics fit together and make sense? Is it that men are better at the job and therefore get more opportunities at the higher levels? Or is it that men do better in charge?

Journey through writing the book

The writing of this book, after its inception, went insanely quick. It was as if a switch had been flicked with my interest and I couldn't get enough of writing it. I started with the history of gender inequality and I truly think that this led me to have a greater, and deeper understanding of the injustices that have come before us. I wanted to get a feel for how far we have come in this fight which then showed me how long we have to go before we can say that we have achieved true equality. I explored how genders had fared throughout the ages, focusing my attention on Britain's experience. The people who helped to shape and develop our country may be gone, but the building blocks that they constructed very much remain, whether for the good or the bad. We have been left with a story of triumphs and of failures, of justice and injustice, or equality and inequality.

I then explored possibly my area of expertise: academic differences between genders in children. I already had preconceived ideas as to what I thought those differences were, so I tried to put those to one side so that I could start writing with a clean slate and no prejudices. The academic differences that I found did in fact tie into the ideas that I had established prior to writing. It's no secret that boys and girls are different, but that should never mean that you don't try to abolish those differences in terms of academics. We can't just ignore that boys underperform; we need to find ways to ensure that the gap is minimal – if not non-existent.

I began to write about the aspirational differences and thought it imperative at this point to talk to the children themselves, to discover their thoughts on gender equality. Not their own gender equality, but more what they could see around them. I wanted to understand their cognition of the world around them in terms of gender, and what they picked up astounded me. Our students are far more in tune with the outside world than we sometimes give them credit for. I established that children generally don't believe that specific careers are only suitable for certain genders, but they do believe there are differences between genders that make them slightly more inclined to go a certain way. This just emphasises the point that we do need to guide these pupils, because it's so easy to slip into the trap of appeasing others over ourselves.

Finally, I thought it crucial to talk about the pressures that our students face outside of the classroom. Some of these pressures were generated from my own experiences and what I've seen; others from conversations I've had with parents, teachers and the students themselves. The pressures that surround our pupils all the time are huge. It will only be through awareness and education that our students will know that they don't have to be the person that society tells them to be. Mental health issues stem from many things, one of which is not feeling like a part of something, not feeling normal, not feeling accepted. In our time, it's so important that we make them understand that they are part of something and will remain part of it until they find themselves settled.

Points that the book raises

The book raises several points that have been considered but now need to be actioned. Inequality in the workplace is a huge problem in the modern day. In the past, as we have seen, unfair workloads and inequality in the home were common. However, in our society – wherein adults of any gender perform the same jobs – there should not still be injustice and prejudice. In schools, it is our job to educate the children not to just accept what has come before them, but rather to spark the idea in their mind that it is not fair, and it can be changed.

Another implication is that our society is still building these gender norms. Ideas of how people should behave in order to fit into one of two categories. It is time that, as a society, we need to accept that there are no longer two columns to consider. Gender is a spectrum, and most people fall somewhere in between the archaic stereotypes of man and woman. We have androgyny and trans, and tomboys and effeminate men. All of these terms that our children are hearing every day are their norm, so why are we still limiting our students to fit into centuries-old ideals of how they should behave just because of the genitalia that they were born with?

One of the biggest influences on the children in our care is the media. They are constantly bombarded with ideals of how to look, speak, act. There are some brilliant role models out there, and YouTube gives a great platform for children to look up to some really inspiring people; but with that comes risks of those who are not great models for students, and those who also affirm those unrealistic expectations for our students. It has to have an effect on them; there's no way that our students could not be affected by the world that is around them every way we turn. And no, we shouldn't wrap them in cotton wool, but they do need to be made aware that the people they see on the screen or hear on the radio are not always the people they should aspire to be.

Many teachers unfortunately do have preconceived ideas about how genders should behave in their classrooms. Many don't realise that they are in fact reaffirming someone's gender by calling a girl 'darling', and a boy 'mate'. Teachers need to recognise where, in their practice, they are reaffirming these gender stereotypes, and cut them out. Girls will start to show more confidence; boys will start to show more interest in their studies. We are trivialising their individuality by bracketing them into boys and girls when it is just not needed. They will find their place, but that shouldn't be decreed by what gender they are.

The blueprint of life has been a common theme throughout this book for a good reason. We all have one. A predestined path that we are supposed to follow in order to do well at school and succeed in life as a man or as a woman. There is no escaping the fact that society will expect our children to go a certain path, but there should be another way shown to them too.

So what next?

This book's purpose was to be a catalyst for change. It was to make educators everywhere think about the world that we want our students to grow up in – the students that we help to raise from age 3 all the way up to whenever they deem their education is over.

I want you to imagine a world wherein equality is pure for all genders. A world where there is no difference in pay, no misogyny, no sexual harassment, no unfair opportunities. It may seem strange for us to imagine such a world because we don't know it. Those things just seem natural to us. But they're not natural at all. It's not natural for someone to be treated differently from others because of the colour of their skin, or their religion, or their sexuality, or their gender. It's not natural that people just accept that this is normal.

I want my students to grow up in a world that doesn't think this is normal. They, and we, have the power to change what has been centuries of oppression for so many people.

By implementing strategies in the classroom that I have discussed, hopefully more of your students will see the injustices that we all face.

We want our students happy, healthy and unique. What would be the fun in having a class split down the middle where one side behaves one way, and another side behaves another? We don't have that now, so the next thing, looking forward, is that we appreciate our students for the individuals that they are, rather than the genders that they were reputedly predisposed to develop.

Now that we've busted some of the myths discussed earlier, teachers should feel confident going into their classrooms and teaching equality in a positive and honest way. I know that after implementing the lesson ideas in my own teaching, my pupils have grown in confidence and are able to understand that their gender doesn't define who they are as a person. I want teachers to go into their classroom armed with the knowledge that while boys and girls may be biologically different, socially it's not so clear.

Most of all, what I want next is that the generation of students that we have now and that we will have in ten years will leave school knowing that you have believed in them, that they have the power to change things that they don't like, and that they are not a product of the 50/50 split in the world but rather an explosion of the cosmos wherein tiny particles have joined together to make someone that is one of a kind.

As teachers, you have the power to make them believe that of themselves. Be their gender hero.

There's not much left to say

Ending this book is quite bittersweet. I don't want to let it go, yet on the other hand I want people to explore this book and magpie ideas left, right and centre. It has been a journey. A journey wherein I've learnt a lot about myself both as a person and as an educator. I started out with no real clue as to where it was going to go, but I was driven all the way by the love I have for my profession and the brilliant educators that I have been taught by and that I know. It's a profession where you have to be a teacher, a doctor, a counsellor, an athlete and an Olympic medal-worthy coffee-drinker all the time to achieve the best that you can for the children.

I love my job and I love that I learn new things every single day. What I don't love is that I know what kind of world I am sending the children out to when they leave me and the safety of my classroom. On the last day of term, I cry without fail. But I don't cry out of sadness but out of the sheer happiness that I feel knowing that I am sending them out into this world with an arsenal of beliefs in themselves and the world.

By reading this book, I'm sure you will have a passion for that too. The passion for wanting to be a teacher, a doctor, a counsellor, an athlete and an Olympic medal-worthy coffee-drinker all the time. The passion for wanting to create the next generation of thinkers and doers.

I know that my students will go on to achieve great things, and yours will too. We guide them and teach them about everything that they need to know. Just make sure we don't leave anything out. I believe in equality, I believe in justice and I believe that my students should be who they want to be.

I'm going to end with a quote from the one-and-only *Indiana Jones*.

'It's time to ask yourself what you believe.'

Bibliography

Aldrich, R. (2011) *School and society in Victorian Britain: Joseph Payne and the new world of education*. Abingdon: Routledge.

Arnold, M. (1908) *Reports on elementary schools 1852–1882*. London: The Stationery Office.

ASCL (2018) 'Nine out of 10 headteachers say social media is damaging the mental health of pupils', ASCL website. Available at: www.ascl.org.uk/news-and-views/news_news-detail.nine-out-of-10-headteachers-say-social-media-is-damaging-the-mental-health-of-pupils.html [Accessed 22 April 2018].

Bailey, R. (2011) *Letting children be children*. Department for Education. London: The Stationery Office.

Barker, M. and Duschinsky, R. (2012) 'Sexualisation's four faces: sexualisation and gender stereotyping in the *Bailey Review*', *Gender and Education* 24 (3) pp. 303–310.

Bovey, A. (2015) *Women in medieval society*. [Online] Available at: www.bl.uk/the-middle-ages/articles/women-in-medieval-society [Accessed 15 January 2018].

Brechet, C. (2013) 'Children's gender stereotypes through drawings of emotional faces: do boys draw angrier faces than girls?', *Sex Roles* 68 (5–6) pp. 378–389.

Carnevali, F. and Strange, J.-M. (eds) (2014) *20th century Britain: economic, cultural and social change.* 3rd edn. Abingdon: Routledge.

Charlton, K. (2007) *Education in Renaissance England.* 2nd edn. Abingdon: Routledge.

Coltrane, S. (1996) *Family man: fatherhood, housework, and gender equity.* 2nd edn. Oxford: Oxford University Press.

Crafts, N., Gazeley, I. and Newell, A. (eds) (2007) *Work and pay in 20th century Britain.* Oxford: Oxford University Press.

D'Angour, A. (2013) 'Plato and play: taking education seriously in Ancient Greece', *American Journal of Play* 5 (3), pp. 293–307.

Department for Education (2017). *School workforce in England: November 2016.* London: The Stationery Office.

Department for Education (2018). *School workforce in England: November 2017.* London: The Stationery Office.

Friedman, A. T. (1985) 'The influence of humanism on the education of girls and boys in Tudor England', *History of Education Quarterly* 25 (1–2) pp. 57–70.

Frith, E. (2017) *Social media and children's mental health: a review of the evidence.* London: Education Policy Institute. Available at www.epi.org.uk/wp-content/uploads/2018/01/Social-Media_Mental-Health_EPI-Report.pdf [Accessed 22 April 2018].

Goodson, I. F. (2005) *Learning, curriculum and life politics.* Oxon: Routledge.

Gordon, P., Aldrich, R. and Dean, D. (1991) *Education and policy in England in the twentieth century.* London: The Woburn Press.

Jeffreys, B. (2018) 'Why do schools have a massive pay gap?', *BBC News* website. Available at: www.bbc.co.uk/news/education-43460998 [Accessed 12 June 2018].

Kramarae, C. and Spender, D. (2000) *Routledge international encyclopedia of women: global women's issues and knowledge.* London: Routledge.

Lowe, R. (ed.) (2012a) *Education and the Second World War: studies in schooling and social change.* 2nd edn. Abingdon: Routledge.

Lowe, R. (2012b) *Education in the post-war years: a social history.* 2nd edn. Abingdon: Routledge.

McNaughton, G. (2000) *Rethinking gender in early childhood.* Sydney: Allen & Unwin.

Marks, J., Bun, L. C. and McHale, S. M. (2009) 'Family patterns of gender role attitudes', *Sex Roles* 61 (3–4) pp. 221–234.

Norton, E. (2016) *Tudor girls and education.* [Online] Available at: tudortimes.co.uk/guest-articles/tudor-girls-and-education [Accessed 24 January 2018].

Ofsted (2018a) *Ofsted's gender pay gap report 2017.* London: The Stationery Office. Available at: www.gov.uk/government/publications/ofsted-gender-pay-gap-report-and-data-2017 [Accessed 12 June 2018].

Ofsted (2018b) *Annual report and accounts 2017–18.* London: The Stationery Office. Available at: assets.publishing.service.gov.uk/government/uploads/system/uploads/attachment_data/file/725797/Ofsted_Annual_Report___Accounts_2017-18_-_WEB-160718.pdf [Accessed 2 August 2018].

Olley, J. (2017) 'How a Somali-born girl became a referee of men's football in England – the remarkable story of Jawahir Roble', *Evening Standard* website. Available at: www.standard.co.uk/sport/football/how-a-somaliborn-girl-became-a-referee-of-men-s-football-in-england-the-remarkable-story-of-jawahir-a3654736.html [Accessed 14 June 2018].

Orme, N. (2006) *Medieval schools: from Roman Britain to Renaissance England.* London: Yale University Press.

Picard, L. (2009) *Education in Victorian Britain.* [Online] Available at: www.bl.uk/victorian-britain/articles/education-in-victorian-britain [Accessed 24 January 2018].

Roberts, J. (2018) 'Ofsted refuses to say what officials did to earn five-figure bonuses', *TES* website. Available at: www.tes.com/news/ofsted-refuses-say-what-officials-did-earn-five-figure-bonuses [Accessed 1 September 2018].

Rust, J., Golombok, S., Hines, M., Johnston, K., Golding, J. and the ALSPAC Study Team (2000) The role of brothers and sisters in the gender development of preschool children, *Journal of Experimental Child Psychology* 77 (4) pp. 292–303.

Sanderson, M. (1995) *Education, economic change and society in England 1780–1870 (New studies in economic and social history).* 2nd edn. Cambridge: Cambridge University Press.

Segall, W. E. (2006) *School reform in a global society.* Oxford: Rowman and Littlefield Publishers.

Tomlinson, S. (2005) *Education in a post-welfare society.* 2nd edn. Maidenhead: Open University Press.

Trueman, C. N. (2015) *Medieval education.* [Online] Available at: historylearningsite.co.uk/medieval-england/medieval-education [Accessed 15 January 2018].

Turan, S. (2011) 'Plato's concept of education in Republic and Aristotle's concept of education in *Politics', Education and Science* 36 (162) pp. 31–38.

Whitby, K., Lord, P., O'Donell, S. and Grayson, H. (2006) *Dips in performance and motivation: a purely English perception?* London: National Foundation for Educational Research.

Worth, J., De Lazzari, G. and Hillary, J. (2017) *Teacher retention and turnover research: interim report.* Slough: NFER. Available at: www.nfer.ac.uk/publications/NUFS03/NUFS03.pdf [Accessed 12 June 2018].

Wrigley, C. (2009) *A companion to early twentieth-century Britain.* 2nd edn. Chichester: Blackwell.

Acknowledgements

Writing this book has been my biggest achievement to date. It would not have been possible without the support of my current school and the teacher at the helm, Debbie Eccles. Working in a school that values the children above everything else is not something that comes gratis, but that is what Victoria CP does. I have been able to try new teaching techniques and explore new ideas because the school is all about changing for the times.

I'd also like to say a huge thanks to Ross Morrison McGill and the team at Teacher Toolkit, without whom I would not have had such an enormous platform to share my views. I've always wanted to write, but I've never known where to start. Teacher Toolkit is a brilliant place to start your writing career, giving you a non-judgemental way to explore topics and ideas in a safe way.

Thank you to my partner, my family and my friends, who have all opened my eyes to how people can think and feel differently about this important topic. And thank you again to my partner for putting up with me reading bits of the book out loud to make sure they were right!

Finally, I'd like to thank the people who make my job worth it every single day: the children for whom I have written the book. Every day, I see the future being established within the four walls of my classroom, and I want their future to be free from bias and prejudice so that they can achieve what they are capable of.

Index

D

data 8, 13, 48–50, 62, 66, 72–73, 80, 94–95, 126, 140

Department for Education 140

drama 11, 20, 60, 84–85, 145, 155, 176

E

exams 39, 75, 99

expectations 13, 20–21, 32, 92, 138, 141–142, 144, 157, 170, 173, 189

F

family 18, 22, 25, 27, 32, 36, 41, 67, 77, 80, 100, 114–115, 123–125, 134–135, 141, 143, 146, 163–164, 168–173, 181

film 9, 14, 146, 155–160, 180

Foundation Phase 22, 53, 71–74, 162, 174

further education – *see* university

G

gender pay gap 135, 140–141, 179

I

identity 166, 168–170, 175, 180, 186

J

jobs 12, 14, 19, 21, 25, 27, 33, 39, 40, 42, 50, 57, 62–63, 68, 72, 77, 80, 83, 86, 88, 91, 99, 100, 102–141, 149, 156, 169, 172–174, 178, 185–187, 189, 192

K

Key Stage 1 79–82, 102–104

Key Stage 2 67, 70–73, 92–93, 104–115

L

LGBTQ 166, 172

literacy 28, 30, 38, 41, 52, 72, 74, 80, 126

M

maths 13, 28, 36, 44, 48, 52–53, 64, 74–76, 80, 84, 92, 111, 175

music 18, 22–23, 29, 34, 87, 155–156, 160–161, 180

O

Ofsted 41, 141

P

parents 7, 10, 14–16, 18, 23, 31, 33–34, 40, 67, 71–72, 75, 77–78, 80, 82, 89, 91, 97–98, 100, 102, 105, 107–109, 124, 132, 134–135, 139, 144–149, 154, 158, 160, 162, 166, 168–176, 180–181, 188. *See also* family

pay gap – *see* gender pay gap

PE 56, 83, 92, 98, 118–119, 138, 186

peer pressure 144, 146, 161–168, 180–183

U

uniform 47, 75, 151

See also clothing

university 11, 27–29, 34, 36, 77, 97, 99, 105, 120, 186

W

writing 22–25, 33, 50–52, 65, 70, 72, 90, 97, 131, 148, 176, 186–188